OLD ROADS, NEW FRIENDS

Reflections on Walking the Camino de Santiago

Other books by Adam G. Fleming

Fiction

White Buffalo Gold

The Stetson Jeff Adventures (With Justin Fike):

Beatdown in Bangkok
Mayhem in Marrakesh
Pandemonium in Paradise
Stetson Jeff Adventures Vol. 1 with A Very Stetson Christmas

The Satchel Pong Chronicles:

Satchel Pong and the Great Migration
Satchel Pong and the Search for Emil Ennis
Antoinette Xho and the Sky Dwellers
St. Kipstofer and the Miraculous Yarkarma
The Prophets of Doom and the Leaping Hedgehog

Non-Fiction

The Art of Motivational Listening
How to Make a Positive Cultural Impact
Old Roads, New Friends

Poems and Flash Fiction

Vortex Street

Visit www.adamgfleming.com for information on how to acquire these fine titles as e-books, audiobooks or to order autographed copies.

OLD ROADS, NEW FRIENDS

Reflections on Walking the Camino de Santiago

By Adam G. Fleming

Friendly Hedgehog Books

Goshen, Indiana

Old Roads, New Friends:

Reflections on Walking the Camino de Santiago

Cover and interior design by
Pledge Communications,
Maadi, Cairo, Arab Republic of Egypt
www.pledgecommunications.com

ISBN: 978-1-958622-03-2

Dedication

For my dear friend Slobodanka "Sammy" Blagojevic, who tattooed the title of this book on her wrist even before I began to write it.

Acknowledgements

This book would not have been possible without the pilgrims who walked, talked, and ate with me, and the volunteers who serve on the Camino. First, I want to thank the five who were with me at dinner when the title of this book leapt from my lips: Sammy from Germany, Joe from Ireland, Britt and Jasmine from The Netherlands, Sabrina from Germany. I also want to mention everyone else, in the order I met them. Sara from Belgium, albergue host in Porto; Don Gabriel from Bali/The Netherlands; Jack, Kaya and Max from Hawaii, USA; Fernando from Spain, host at Monastery at Vairão; Riccardo from Italy; Igor and Gustavo from Brazil/Portugal; Carlos from Venezuela/London; Fernanda and Jacinto, hosts in Lugar do Corgo, and Christian from Germany at Casa da Fernanda; Maya and Esse from Finland; The Instagram model and her boyfriend from Los Angeles; The Mexican guy on the bridge; Alberto from Brazil/Lisbon; Hugo from Porto; The Kid from Poland; Carmen, host in Armenteira, who pointed me to vespers; the monks and nuns in Armenteira; Jonas from Brno, Czech Republic; Don Jose, Alfonso and Debee, at the chapel in Mouzo; Roberta from Iowa, USA; Virginie The Wanderer from Lyons, France; Sven and Alex from Germany.

Old friends and acquaintances who walked the Camino before me: Myron Bontrager; Dean Rhodes; Jonathan and Carol Bornman, my debriefing partners, kindred spirits in a life of adventure, and bold eaters of ice cream for breakfast.

Everyone who supported my work as CEO of Evergreen Leaders since 2014, and the members of the board: Tim, Julie, and Kim, who agreed I should take a sabbatical from that work and approved the budget.

My wife Megan, who agreed to be my best friend in 1998; who has never wavered in her commitment to our friendship; who sent me all over the world before she sent me to Porto; who finally edited this book with a tenacity for quality and a passion for the Chicago Manual of Style. Megan, how could I write anything about friendship and not mention you?

Foreword

By Dr. Jonathan Bornman, social anthropologist, filmmaker

March 2022

Dear reader,

What you have here is a pilgrim's collection of thoughts and ideas upon which he has ruminated while walking along a path, sometimes alone and often with other travelers. Making a pilgrimage on El Camino de Santiago de Compostela has perhaps only one rule—walk your own camino. My camino, walked just two months prior to Adam's, was a spiritual pilgrimage. My internal understanding was that each step of the 315 km of the Camino Primitivo route was a step towards Jesus. Except for a few hours I walked the path alone, enjoying conversation and fellowship in the evening with other pilgrims. It was surprising how important these camino friends became to me and how much I enjoyed meeting up with them every few days. These new friends became my community. We checked on each other asking, "did you see so and so?" or "how are your feet?" It seemed that most understood the rule—walk your own camino—and we were all better for it.

At first, I gave nearly all my attention to following the yellow arrows that guide pilgrims along the path. But as days went by, following the markers became almost second nature. Eventually, sometime in my second week of walking, the idea crossed my mind that maybe something much more profound was going on. A line from a poem I did not even know that I knew came to mind, "there is no path, paths are made by walking"[i]. The first pilgrim to walk El Camino Primitivo was King Alphonse II sometime in the late 800s; since then, pilgrims have followed the route he took. I assumed that I too was just following the path, and then came the thought that if there were no pilgrims, the path would soon be overgrown and disappear. Pilgrims like me are not following the path, but rather we are creating it. Our intention to set out on pilgrimage puts our bodies in motion and our feet take steps to keep up with our spirits. Adam conceptualizes *old roads and new friends* as a creative space where new things and new friendships spring into being. French philosopher Michael de Certeau[ii] says that these social spaces only exist as long as there are people moving their bodies through that space. I propose that these essays are the fruit of this "old roads, new friends" social space. Reading them now, outside of that space that only exists when you are walking El Camino, these essays seem to come from another world. Even the strange new vocabulary Adam has created is only strange because we are trying to peer into a space that no longer exists.

The invitation to write this foreword comes because of a long friendship. Adam and I first met at church, but our friendship began when he came to visit our family in Senegal in 2005. Part of the time was spent just sharing life together, and part of the trip was a journey along the Atlantic coast, exploring rocks and sea. We visited with stone carvers, and we spent hours talking about anything and everything. That journey set the tone for a lifelong relationship. Sometimes we have gone years without encountering one another. Recently a funeral brought me to Goshen, where Carol and I stayed in Adam and Megan's home for over a week. We are old friends, now venturing over new roads.

My last day on the camino, I walked entirely alone. I did not even glimpse any of my new friends. Approaching the city of Santiago and walking the last hour in an urban setting was disorienting after hundreds of kilometers in the countryside. I got a bit lost but eventually found the street that leads into the grand plaza in front of the cathedral. Entering the plaza, suddenly I heard clapping, then people calling my name. In the center of the plaza were three of my friends from the trail. As I approached, they began to cheer and finally greeted me with huge hugs! Old Roads, New Friends offers a glimpse of the vitality of life on El Camino and perhaps an invitation to live on pilgrimage wherever we find ourselves, if we so choose. Walk your own camino and cheer for everyone as they arrive!

Preface

"No one leaves his character behind when going on a journey." Nigerian proverb

The Camino

The remains of St. James, the apostle of Jesus Christ who brought Christianity to the Iberian Peninsula, are said to be buried in the cathedral at the city of Santiago de Compostela, in the autonomous Xunta of Galicia, Spain's northwestern-most region, directly north of Portugal.

According to tradition, James began his preaching in the modern-day town of Padrón, 26 km south of Santiago, but was martyred in Roman-occupied Judea, executed by King Herod Agrippa I in the year 44 A.D. Legend suggests that James' corpse was caught up by angels, put on a boat without sailors, miraculously drifted across the Mediterranean, beyond Gibraltar and north along the Atlantic to Padrón, where his bones were entombed in rock. About 800 years later the remains of St. James were discovered by Alfonso II, king of Asturias (a nation which covered much of the region in northwestern Spain of modern times).

Whether one believes these legends about St. James or not today, the discovery by Alfonso II baptized the city of Santiago de Compostela as a popular destination for pilgrims, who have been hiking, riding horseback, boating, and even cycling and running to arrive in Santiago, making their penance along the Way, arriving to seek indulgences, enlightenment, a miracle healing or some other sort of truth or clarity or purpose, and in modern times simply enjoying a well-catered walking holiday. This has been going on, sometimes more and sometimes less, for as long as 1100 years.

Unlike Mecca, which is open to pilgrims or hajji who are adherents of Islam, the Camino de Santiago (Way of St. James) attracts people of any spiritual stripe, inviting them to visit the city. One can even attend a mass at the Cathedral (but please don't take communion unless you are a Catholic— if you don't know that you are, then you're not). Before the Covid-19 pandemic began, more than 1000 people per day were arriving in Santiago at the end of a long road, each one having traveled at least 100 km but often 800 km or farther, to complete their pilgrimages.

The Way of St. James, or Camino de Santiago, is the most popular Christian pilgrimage in the world. Of course, people go to Jerusalem as well, but that's not known as a hiking excursion. You just fly there and take a bus tour of the Holy Lands.

There are many routes to Santiago, with accommodations which make the hiking possible and affordable to many while eliminating the necessity of carrying tents and food. Hostels or albergues provide inexpensive lodging at convenient intervals, and many restaurants along the route offer a pilgrim blue-plate special, an inexpensive but high-calorie meal.

Travelers who are in-between jobs, retired, or recently graduated sometimes hike from as far away as Germany, Holland, and Italy, walking all the way across France and northern Spain to complete the journey. The Camino Frances is the most popular camino, beginning in St. Jean in the French Pyrenees, and the Camino Portugués is the second most popular. It begins in Lisbon, but due to time constraints many people begin this Camino in Porto, or even in Valença or Tui on the Portuguese/Spanish border. There is no correct way to get to Santiago.

I made the pilgrimage in November of 2021 from Porto, Portugal, to Santiago de Compostela, walking approximately 300 km (186 miles) in 15 days. By way of introduction, what is more important than what happened and where it happened and how far I walked each day is the question: Why?

Pilgrims all have their own reasons, and, as Fernanda says, "it's your Camino, so do it your own Way." For me, it was a spiritual retreat, a sabbatical from my work as a nonprofit executive. I was seeking a break from the grind and enough space to consider what I wanted my focus to be for the coming five to seven years. I did find some answers to that question. However, that self-exploration and self-discovery isn't the focus of this book. This is not an autobiographical work as much as it is an essay, an attempt to put words to things I found were difficult to explain, along a more universal theme. Many books have been written about the Camino; I believe this theme is both more interesting to the public and more worthy of writing about for the public benefit. I am not under any illusions that the public cares much about the twists and turns of my personal career decisions.

How did I find this theme, and what is it? I expected to, and did, walk quite a lot of the journey alone. That was the point of the pilgrimage in the first place. Because I went during the off-season and traveled a less-popular route, sometimes I walked an entire day without even seeing another pilgrim; even though I am an extrovert the solitude sparkled like morning dew on the vineyards. But as I walked this ancient path, I also encountered many strangers who became new friends; we became close in an astonishingly short time. We met on the path or in the albergues, cafes, and restaurants. We walked, talked, ate, and drank together, (it was a holy communion) and often even slept in the same room, listening to each other snoring.

One evening at dinner with Sammy, Joe, Sabrina, Britt, and Jasmine, I raised my glass and said I wanted to make a toast. They gave me their attention. I said only these six words: "To old roads and new friends." I hadn't given it much thought. I suppose it was a moment of poetic inspiration.

"That sums it up perfectly," they said. Everyone raised their glasses. "To old roads and new friends. Cheers."

I can be kind of dense. It was a few days later when I realized the theme for my journey was friendship. Because I expected to walk alone, this surprised me more than it should have; I've known for years that friendship is one of my top core values. It was Joe who said, "Adam, you're the friendliest guy on the Camino." I know myself well enough to say this is what I would both hope and expect to hear. I nodded and agreed; it's accurate. Joe, they said, was the funniest guy on the Camino. (They haven't read my satirical novels yet. But to be fair, Joe is a more animated storyteller than I am, and has a twinkle in his eye which indicates that he has told and heard many a story in Irish pubs.) Sammy was 'Mama Camino'. And everyone else, too, had a special place in the community.

In retrospect, I expected to find out something new or different about myself, perhaps find in the experience some kind of radical shift, not just in my career direction, but that I was going to uncover a new self that would surprise everyone. You let go of your identity to walk the Camino. I wasn't there to be a cross-cultural coaching skills trainer, like I was when I went to live in Egypt. I wasn't there to be a business or life or leadership coach. Or novelist. Or dad and husband. I was just there being me. So, the things that are core to my character came to the forefront as I was just another pilgrim, just another guy on the Camino, but not really just another guy: I was the friendliest guy. When someone else said it, I knew it was true! Of course, I was. That's exactly who I am when you take away all the stuff I do. If I ever walk it again, I will be that again. That is who I am: one of the friendliest guys you ever met, on the Camino or anywhere else. It is the thing that people recognize in me when I am not trying to be anything but myself.

I arrived in Santiago with Britt and Jasmine, whom I had caught up with about 12 km from the end of the Way, a pleasant surprise. Aside for some down time due to a prank I played on Britt, at Jasmine's prompting, we hurtled toward the Cathedral together. When we came around the corner, Sammy was waiting at the cathedral for us. She had gotten my words tattooed on her wrist:

Old Roads, New Friends.

It was stunning. To see my words tattooed on someone else's skin is the sort of experience I would not have dared to dream about. It is a once-in-a-lifetime honor. It is better than a Pulitzer Prize. I knew this would have to be the title of my book. What I meant when I blurted out that toast would require more thought!

Every essay has a thesis, it is an attempt to elaborate upon a theorem: I observed that something happens on old roads which allows us to establish friendships with people in just a few moments of walking that leaves us feeling as if we have known one another since before we were born, like twins who have curled up together in utero, a sensation that we are souls who met in that place where souls wait for a conception to occur, (if such a place exists, as depicted in the animated movie *Soul*) as if we always knew we'd end up in the same place at the same time in November of 2021 or whatever time it was that we were somehow predestined to show up there at the crossroads where relationships are formed; at Fernanda's house, for example. We are technically new friends, but we don't feel that way at all. What is this phenomenon? Is it universal, or was it only my experience? What does it take, how do we get there? How do we reproduce it? And then there are the moments of *sonder*[3], when our complex lives bump up against another soul whose life is equally intriguing and complex, and for whatever reason, we don't become friends. Why? What is so great about being alone, and how can we walk alone but not feel lonely?

And what is a friend, anyway?

The term "essay" is identical to the French word for "attempt or try". I am attempting to explain this phenomenon, to discuss these themes, hoping to figure it out as I write cold rough drafts, go for walks in the park, dream about returning to the Camino, and shuffle through multiple edits. But be forewarned, I suspect there are mysteries here I cannot adequately explain. Friendship is something we all need, but I don't believe it's well understood.

A few additional notes of introduction before we get rolling: I will introduce my friends haphazardly, as I did above with mentions of Fernanda, Sammy, Joe, Britt, Jasmine, and Sabrina. In this way, you will meet them as I did, discovered in casual moments along the journey, but I will write about them also as if they were always there, as if you always knew who they were. Which, of course, you did. They have been known, each in their own worlds, since their birth; they are humans just like the humans you have known since your own birth.

For those who are looking for all the linear, factual details about how I trained for the Camino and selected my gear, what happened on the Camino, how much hiking I did each day, where I went, who I met on what day and where they are from, I've put these things in three appendices. Feel free to skip to that section if your primary interest is in the how-to aspect of the Camino de Santiago, or if you feel that the linear background will give you context to better engage the essays before you dive into chapter one.

Chapter 1

Old Roads

The sea is the oldest road.
All roads lead to Rome.

The oldest roads, which were at one time slick new highways for the most adventurous human beings, were easily forgotten as the Autobahn century crescendoed toward the panic of Y2K. The most adventurous took to the air, like Charles Lindberg and Amelia Earhart; or to space, for example, Neil Armstrong and Christa McAuliffe. Once they had done this, explorers fell down the rabbit hole of the fastest road ever: the Internet, connecting us via the mobile phone, foreseen by writers like Ivan Illich in his book *Deschooling Society* and in futuristic fiction, like Star Trek. While the various uses for this newest of all superhighways, for better or worse, were pioneered by everyone from V.P. Al Gore to Weird Al Yankovic to Al Qaeda, the reality is that almost every one of us went down that rabbit hole without asking many questions about the hazards of said method of "travel".

But even as the speed of our travel accelerated to this pace, spiritually hungry folks and artists like me began looking for ways to slow down. The greatest social insights and creative inspirations are not found in a hurry. The spark of innovation does not come while we are trying. It comes when we are in the shower, or as we drift off to sleep, or as we walk by the 172nd milepost. Toward the end of the last century, some famous artists began discovering the inner delight and physical wonder of walking toward Santiago; Paulo Coelho went on pilgrimage in 1986, Shirley MacLaine in 1994, and finally in 2010 Emilio Estevez produced a film called The Way, starring his father Martin

Sheen, further popularizing the Camino de Santiago for a new generation of pilgrims. Estevez resisted the pressure to make it a fast-paced adventure film. He knew that The Camino is about slowing down.

Old Roads: They carry us toward destinations which have been and still are valuable places to go, but they do so in a less harried fashion. It requires intentionality for us to slow down enough to use the old roads. Most pilgrims on the Camino arrive in Santiago the same way St. Francis of Assisi did in the 1200s—on foot. New roads cut corners, invite us to travel at maximum velocity, urge us to reach our destination without taking in the quiet country, get us somewhere without losing a minute, permit us to toss our rubbish along the shoulder, and allow us to ignore the sins against the planet of our littering without immediate consequences. (Whenever the Camino followed a major highway for a few miles, I noticed a marked increase in trash, and found that the Portuguese and Spanish are no better than Americans in this respect, while in their automobiles.) On a new road, we're not living in the moment when we travel, we're trying to get to the next moment.

On old roads we are more able, as Saint James said, *to be quick to listen, slow to speak, and slow to become angry.*[4] By contrast, on new roads, we're tempted to lose ourselves in road rage. Perhaps this is the best way to tell what kind of road you're traveling, old or new. How quickly do you become angry? Not once on the Camino did I experience road rage! Never did I say to another person "would you kindly get the heck out of my way?" On an old road, you have all day to get where you're going. A caveat: ironically, I did find myself annoyed when the Camino went along a highway, and I saw all the trash. I wanted those forest paths to extend all the way from Porto to Santiago without interruption by whooshing delivery trucks and zipping commuters.

If the sea is the oldest road, the Internet is the newest. There is no application I use more on a daily basis than Zoom. This year (2021), I have traveled via the newest, fastest road to visit my trainees and clients in Abu Dhabi, Aleppo, Alexandria, Asyut, Barcelona, Belize, Cairo, California, Chicago, Cornwall, Dubai, and that's just covering places whose names begin with the first four letters of the alphabet.

Once, in Thailand I was talking to a guy named Chase, who told me that a good photographer zooms with his feet. In terms of photography this means to approach or distance oneself from the subject by moving the camera physically, rather than relying on the technological ability of the camera itself to zoom in or out, or any additional telescopic lens. Not only is this an excellent principle in photography, but it also serves as an excellent analogy for old roads as well. Zooming in or out while we frame and reframe our own lives is best done with our feet.

While walking, we don't zoom, in the sense of zooming being a rapid act. This kind of zooming is not about hasty travel, it is about deliberate positioning. For the remainder of the book, when I say *zoom*, I mean the slowing down kind, unless I add the word ‹application› to indicate the Internet communication tool.

Put yourself in the frame. Walk toward something. Walk away from something else. Once you find a place of not-knowing, you'll get a close up of one part of your life and a wide angle shot of the rest of it, all at the same time.

Zooming with your feet is more than an instruction for photography. It is a life practice that somehow allows us the opportunity to reexamine who we are and what we are about. When I say zoom with your feet, it is metaphorical, but on the Camino, it is also literal.

Chase was right. Zoom with your feet.

To get a better picture, to find focus and clarity, you will need an old road and enough time disconnected from your work, from the things that you do, so that you can slow down long enough to *be*.

Things to get away from:

Email
Texts and Messages
Social Media
Other peoples' advertising
Binge-worthy shows
Podcasts

Memes
Input (more memes, satire)
Input (political and economic hype)
Input (religious hype)
Input (other people are stupid, join my tribe)
Input.
Output, too: Marketing, posting.

Why get away from output? You cannot just BE while showing everyone else what a great life of BEING you are currently living. Sharing posts is Doing. I consider what I call "Instagram modeling" as a major distraction of being on a pilgrimage. This must be tempered by the reminder that each person chooses their own Camino.

Zooming with your feet requires, builds, and delivers patience. There is no point in hurrying; each day's trouble will suffice. Thirteen miles is thirteen miles; whether you do it in four hours or six and a half, you will still be tired. It's easy to be impatient, and want to get in more miles, but you will need to rest. You need to find lodging, and the albergues are a perfect place to meet other people, to sit and talk, to sleep, to allow this zooming concept the time it requires if you want to just be... it is easy to make even the simple act of walking a way of *doing*.

In my quest for a place to rest, I never called ahead for a reservation (but I would recommend doing so during the busy season). I merely showed up and asked for a bed. Only once in two weeks did I find this to be a problem, when I passed the center of Tui, hoping to find a place on the quiet edge of town, and found two albergues closed before I located the third— and last— option. I could have slept in a stable, I was tired enough.

One of the principles I live by is *go as far as you can go*. So, rather than turning back, I continued. Using my sketchy Spanish, I asked an old man where the next place to stay was, and he told me that the Camino went to the right. I put my hands beside my head in the universal sign for "sleep" and said *"quiero una cama,"* and the man said to go past the church and turn left to find the way to lodging. In a few more minutes, I

| go as far as you can go |

found a delightful place, Albergue Pallane, with an eager and welcoming hostess. I was the first guest to arrive that day, and I think she was worried there wouldn't be much traffic, as the season was fizzling out. She brought me a few beers, on the house. I taught her the difference between "door" and "gate" in English. To my great pleasure I found that Joe from Ireland was lodging there as well! Had I turned back, I would not have had the pleasure of slamming a massive hamburger and hearing stories of Ireland with Joe that evening. There are few better ways to just be than to have dinner with Joe.

Joe used to work with a company that had a division in Greece. The Greeks, he said, are much more open about some of their observations than the Irish are. One Greek colleague visited the offices in Ireland and noticed one of the ladies.

"Joe," he said later, "There's one woman in your office. She's a real beauty. I mean, you could put her up against anyone in the world. She's an international beauty!"

"Who's that?" Joe asked. He knew, but he didn't let on. It's not that Irish men don't notice the prettiest women, it's just that they would never mention it out loud to another fella.

"You know Amber?"

"Yes," said Joe, surprised.

"The one who wears mismatched clothing?" said the Greek.

"Yes," Joe said, confused.

"The one whose hair is chopped off as if she did it herself, the crooked teeth, the big nose..."

"Yes," said Joe. "She's the real beauty?"

"There's Amber, and then, ...there's the woman who sits *beside* her...," said the Greek.

Joe might have told this story six times in a week and twice on Sundays, and he would have cracked himself up every time. I loved it! Old roads are great places for pointless tales, myths and legends of beautiful men and heroic women, of Greek men and Irish women, of business colleagues and fish restaurant customers and tales of the hazards of using the woods along the trail as one's toilet. In short, some stories fit to be repeated in print, and plenty of stories which are not.

Old roads invite us to go to places people have always wanted to find. They were built because people wanted to get to those places, and they were new roads, for a time. They remained for centuries, and became old, because people still wanted to get to those same locations. Much of early travel was done for economic gain. The seas, and the first paved roads and bridges, despite their cost, greased the skids of prosperity and wealth. But early travelers, perhaps to their surprise, also found their worldview expanded, and their understanding of the spiritual world as well. Sometimes, when all had either been gained, or lost, or the gain had turned into a loss when it was discovered that gain for its own sake was empty, those early travelers used those old roads for expanding their spiritual quest.

Jerusalem, Varanasi, Mecca, Santiago... and out of the way places, like monasteries in Galicia, on Iona, in Nepal and Cambodia...

A road that has taken people somewhere for several thousand years, according to the Lindy effect [5], can be counted on to continue to take people there for a few thousand years more. The Lindy effect is the theory that something that has been around for a certain amount of time can be expected to remain for an equal amount of time into the future. It applies to a road leading to an important port city, or a book like the Bible or the Tao Te Ching, things that are not perishable.

By contrast, you cannot expect a pawpaw fruit that has been ripe for a week to stay ripe for another week. This is why you may never have heard of one of Indiana's native fruit trees. The fruit is delicious, but every tree ripens all its fruit which then rapidly perishes in the same week. Preserving it requires dropping everything when the time comes to harvest. A ripe pawpaw which has been on your counter for two days cannot be expected to last another two days. The Emirates E-11 highway, the road from Abu Dhabi to Dubai, which was completed in 1980, can currently be expected to last another 42 years. That seems about right. When the oil is gone, the E-11 likely will be, too. The temples of consumerism rapidly rise and fall. I learned this in Muscat, Oman: As soon as a new, bigger, better, brighter mall is built, the old mall is forgotten. But soon the emirs invest in another new mall and another new road, and the old malls fall into decay, because there wasn't much of value there in the first place, just consumer goods which fall out of fashion about as quickly as a pawpaw fruit rots in the Indiana forest. And so, life goes on. Few of these new roads will have lasting power or contain any eternal significance. The Apostle James warned us against the hubris of travel on new roads, when he said *"...you who say, 'Today or tomorrow we shall go to such and such a city and spend a year there and engage in business and make a profit.' Yet you do not know what your life will be like tomorrow. You are just* | 𝔇ou are a pawpaw fruit. | *a vapor that appears for a little while and then vanishes away... you boast in your arrogance..."* [6]

Your own life is a New Road. As a perishable entity, you do not get the benefit of the Lindy effect. If you are 80 years old, you cannot expect to live another 80 years! You are a pawpaw fruit.

Nowadays, the oldest roads that remain still go places where people want to go, but they are often used for spiritual journeys. In my county, the old railroad bed from Shipshewana to Goshen, Indiana, has been turned into the Pumpkinvine Nature Trail. This is where I did a lot of my training for the Camino. When the railroad was new, people used it for commerce. Now, it's used for slowing down by walking, running, or cycling. The Amish crowd it three seasons out of the year on Saturday and Sunday afternoons for recreation, and even use it for easy access to the county fair and to their workplaces in local factories, commuting on bicycles. Perhaps you think all Amish travel by buggies. A bike is a lot cheaper in the long run for one man to ride to work. No horse to feed or stable, no harnessing and unharnessing. Still, the Amish do prefer the old roads and old methods of transportation for daily use. Some think it's hypocritical of them to take rides in others' cars, but I say they're on to something.

If it were only for commerce, the railroad bed which became the Pumpkinvine Nature Trail would have disappeared, but thanks to the public easement of land committed to that long-ago railroad and still held by the government, it has been restored for purposes of recreation.

Recreation and spiritual journeys are not so different.

We are re-created when we travel on the old roads. We are, in a sense, born again. Pilgrims want to get to Santiago, but on the way, we find something we didn't expect; we're zooming with our feet, not for purposes of commerce, but to find something–something that was lost as we hurried around on new roads—new perspective on ourselves. What I didn't expect, but should have, was that when you step onto the old Ways, you slow down enough to meet people, and new friends emerge. Surprise!

To travel 1000 miles, one must be in search of something significant, either massive commercial gain or recreational discovery, or both. Now that we have Zoom application calls, businesses are rethinking the idea of doing any business travel to make a sales appointment. That old road called the Autobahn and the airport had better be paved with gold, or better yet with Bitcoin, otherwise we're better off staying put and using the newest road of all: the Internet. And so newer roads are replacing older ones all the time. But they can't replace the oldest ones, because some of us still need to make a journey of 1000 miles.

Confucius said *the journey of 1000 miles begins with a single step.*

Confucius was wrong.

The journey of 1000 miles begins with a spreadsheet.

On April 24, 2021, I started a spreadsheet to track how many miles I walked each day. It was my accountability tool for preparing for the Camino. On November 24, five days after I got home from the Camino, I completed 1000 miles of walking.

> The Journey of
> One Thousand
> Miles Begins with
> a Spreadsheet.

The journey of 1000 miles begins with an agenda, choosing a destination based on a desire and a motive. The journey of 1000 miles can be the agenda. I am a goal-oriented guy. I don't just start books, I finish them. I don't just start hikes, I finish them. We can be agenda-driven either in our arrogance (such as, "I will go to this or that city and make a profit") or in a spirit of curiosity and humility. I am a traveler, not a wanderer. I am not lost, and I go places with purpose. I set out with a desire, and I don't buy the notion that desire is evil— desires are what make us get out of bed in the morning.

There is another saying: *Not all who wander are lost.* Perhaps, but there must be some distinction, so for the purposes of this book: Travelers are people who know where they are going, which could include being intentional about a slow-zooming walkabout. Wanderers are those who are lost, whether they are walking or not. Wanderers don't know what they want. Some of my novels have characters who are wanderers. It is said that a novelist ought to know what his characters want. That is the difference between genre fiction and literary fiction. In genre fiction (fantasy, sci-fi, westerns) one must know the characters' motivations and desires, and move those characters directly toward what they want with plenty of obstacles and pitfalls but without too many bunny trails, or one cannot write energetic, page-turning tales; whereas in literary fiction, where the focus is less about moving the plot along and can instead hinge on character transformation, the author has space to explore the human psyche, including taking time for the main character to wrestle with figuring out what he or she truly wants.

It is almost as difficult to write about a character who doesn't know what he or she wants as it is to be one. Your story, or the story of your life, can drift along, untethered to a motive, unsure of the destination. Some who walk the Camino are Travelers, people who know what they want. Others are Wanderers, people who really and truly don't know. All of us pilgrims, to some extent, think we know what we want, and find out along the way that our desires are shifting, or becoming clearer, as we zoom with our feet. There is hope for the wanderer, but no guarantees, as we shall see.

Few people walk 1000 miles without wanting to get somewhere. But long-haul wanderers do exist, and some of them walk 1000 miles, too, hoping that somehow, they'll find what they're looking for. Perhaps at a certain point a wanderer becomes a nomad, keeping the simplicity of desiring food and a dry, warm bed, as their primary aim. I can't criticize that. It is a simple motive, and some of us can trot along for months or years with the simple desires met and be content. Who am I to criticize people being content with a simple life? But I want more, and I am convinced there's nothing wrong with wanting to make a bigger impact, either.

To clarify further, in my vocabulary, wanderers are not the same as nomads. Nomads and hunter-gatherers know what they want. Not long before I left for the Camino, I came across a Youtube video[7] where a fellow was interviewing some hunter-gatherers of the Hadzabe tribe in Tanzania. He asked the leader what the most important thing in life was.

"Meat," says Socolo. "Meat, honey, corn porridge. Going hunting for baboon. Antelope. Zebra. There, there, there! Look there! Look, look, look! [he points at distant baboons on a high rock, imitates baboon noises] Baboons sleep there. We'll go shoot them, my friend." Socolo lives on old roads and knows that on old roads there are few things more important than getting enough calories, protein, and fat. The purpose, the meaning of life, is as simple as four letters: meat. I noticed that he called the interviewer 'my friend'. Hunting baboons is done in a gang. If meat is the purpose of life, traveling in pursuit with a group of friends is the best way to attain fulfillment.

Wanderers want to go somewhere, but they aren't sure where. They may end up at Santiago, just because a lot of other travelers are using that old road, and the Travelers appear to discover their purpose on the Way. I suppose the wanderers hope that if they wander long enough, they'll find what they're looking for. U2's song *I Still Haven't Found What I'm Looking For* comes to mind as the anthem of the Wanderer. The idea that the Wanderer will find something just because they follow the Travelers' path to Santiago is a false notion. I have seen at least one wanderer frustrated by the experience. Santiago isn't a place so much as an ideal of the discovery or rediscovery of clear purpose. The truth is that the Travelers knew what they wanted beforehand. Then they zoomed with their feet and their desire came into focus. The wanderers left home thinking they'd get what the travelers get. But they were wanderers before they ever left home, and they may run out of money and be forced to return home before they find what they're looking for.

The world is made for people who aren't cursed with self-awareness. – Annie Savoy, in Bull Durham

I wonder if wanderers are nomads who've been cursed with self-awareness.

In her mid-thirties, a woman from France was gone a-wandering. For five months she was on the road, she said, sometimes stopping for a week, and once even for a month, working as a host at one of the albergues. I met her after she arrived in Santiago, and I felt that she was disappointed not to have found whatever she was looking for. We only talked for ten minutes. It was one of those moments where being conversational in French felt like an opportunity for me to give something back, after all I had received. It seemed a very lonely place, to be a wanderer among travelers who were rejoicing to arrive in Santiago, when she felt just as lost as ever. She said that she wanted to continue to Fatima (a location in Portugal where several youths saw visions of Mary in the 1920s). She hadn't found it yet, whatever it was. Maybe she'd get it by the time she got to Fatima. Maybe she wouldn't make it that far, considering that she was running low on funds and wanted to be with family and her *proche* (close ones) at Christmas. If that wasn't lonely enough, she did not speak much Spanish or English. I listened to her story, hoping to give her some encouragement. But I am afraid that for once I spoke platitudes instead of depth. Maybe something I said resonated with her. I'll never know. But I was friendly enough!

We do not migrate instinctively like the Monarch butterfly or the Canada goose. Rarely do you see an animal wandering; rarely are they truly lost. Earlier this year a pair of black-bellied whistling ducks nested in the millrace in Goshen, Indiana. Local birders were checking the black-bellied whistlers off their lists, because their normal northernmost range is Florida, Louisiana, and Texas. Confused, for sure; lost, I don't know. Confused by changing climate patterns, I suppose. Maybe they'll be back again next spring and stay longer. Unlike animals, we don't migrate instinctively. We emigrate. We immigrate. We go out, we come in; there's intent, purpose, emotions, and reasons behind it all. We may be political refugees or move for religious purposes. We may seek better economic opportunity, or just a sunnier spot. We travel. And yes, sometimes we wander. Always, we take our stuff with us.

At the monastery in Armenteira, there are nine nuns and a monk who pray every evening at seven o'clock for pilgrims. They are praying for this French woman too. Whether you are a traveler or a wanderer, and whether that takes the form of a pilgrimage to Santiago or not, they're praying for you every day. I think those elderly nuns know that old roads aren't magical. There aren't guarantees that you'll find that thing you hope to find inside yourself when you wander. The old roads may be places where you can be more spiritually open, more honest with yourself and with others, but they aren't magical. You don't chant a spell and 'find yourself' when you arrive in Santiago. Epiphanies are never guaranteed. The old roads only invite you to search, to make your quest. They don't promise a resolution. And yet you will be re-created. Somehow. The nuns and monks have faith for you if you don't have it for yourself. Change is possible.

Old roads, just like new ones, were designed to take you somewhere specific... and bring you home safely. This does not guarantee that you will arrive or return without feeling lost the entire time.

In the old days, when Francis of Assisi walked to Santiago, you had to go home the same way you came to Santiago. On your feet. I suspect that the return trip would yield many travelers even more clarity. Imagine the familiarity of your surroundings returning as you re-entered your own country: France, Germany, or Italy. You begin to hear your own language spoken again, the closer you get to your home, the more the accents fade, until you get to your own region, your own village, your own mother waits there, ululating, singing songs, warbling in celebration of your return.

Christ modeled for James how to adventure to the outback of the universe. James took Christ's promise that he would be with the Apostles even to the ends of the earth seriously.[1] Consider how close he came to Cape Finisterre to begin his Iberian preaching. The Apostle was only about 50 miles (80 km) from Cape Finisterre (from Latin: finis terrae, literally, The End of The Earth) when he began preaching in Padrón,

---

[1] This reference to the words of Christ in Matthew 28:20 is usually translated as "age" or, "the end of time" or "the end of the world". I realize that this is generally read in terms of the end of time, but I believe that it can also apply to the farthest reaches of geographical space as well, without loss or distortion of meaning.

Spain. To come all the way from Jerusalem to Galicia, James traveled even farther than the Apostle Thomas, who went as far as Tamilakam, the southernmost tip of the Indian subcontinent. James was a traveler and adventurer who sailed the old roads beyond the Pillars of Hercules (Gibraltar), and I'd like to imagine that Saint James used the then-new Roman Road XIX at some point, too.

In the process of zooming with your feet, the destination, while never forgotten, becomes a secondary concern. After all, once you get there, you're only going to turn around and go home. There's not much to do in Santiago besides stand before the cathedral's dizzying height and enjoy the way the church's lines draw your eyes upward until you stare at the clouds drifting far above it... then attend mass, buy a souvenir, have a meal with friends, nurse your aching knees, throw away your worn-out gear, get a cliché tattoo, or something unique and insightful like Sammy did, and get to the bus, train or airport and take a new road out of there.

The destination is not so important. The first concern is to follow the road. The Camino is marked with yellow arrows. You cease to worry about getting to Santiago as you begin to search only for the next arrow. That's living in the moment! At first, when I left Porto, I worried and checked GPS all the time. Am I on the right track? But I learned that the arrows will not lead you astray. The arrows are for travelers who know what they want: they want to go to Santiago. Wanderers are welcome to follow them, too. If you want to get to Santiago, the arrows will show you the way. Finding the internal arrows is more difficult.

On old roads, we have a better chance of finding ourselves, our recreated focus, because we focus on the immediacy of looking for the next arrow, rather than the big picture. We zoom in. At the same time, they take us somewhere significant. We zoom out, we see our whole lives, with the Cathedral at Santiago a metaphor for finding our purpose, our calling. What a huge architectural feat that calling is; something grand and beautiful and pointing to heaven. When we make the spiritual quest, we let go of the arrogance of commerce.

Old roads are a treasure

Of history, with commerce and war,

Of geography, hills and valleys,

Of spirituality, angst and peace,

Of necessity, for reaching destinations far off where family has migrated,

Of humanity. They connect us to being human.

Old roads are for people.

Not for animals, not for angels.

On old roads we find ourselves again human; our gratitude coming in simple bursts of awareness of these blessings:

A sunny day.

A cup of coffee.

Clean, dry underwear.

Something to eat.

> 𝕮lean, dry underwear, the ability to walk.

Having only what is necessary on our backs.

A yellow arrow.

Knowing that our families are supporting us.

Knowing that the nuns are praying for us in Armenteira.

A warm place to sleep.

Clean, dry underwear,

The ability to walk.

I do not want to miss the chance to highlight further my gratitude for the ability to walk. From the time I was about age 25 until age 42 I suffered from gout, undiagnosed for a long time. Doctors don't expect a man of twenty-five to have gout. They don't bother testing for it. Many times, I walked with a cane for three days to three weeks before the fire in my joints abated for a while. The Karamazov brothers were juggling all their knives in my toe, or my ankle, or my knee.

My father had polio as a boy. He appreciated even more than I do the ability to get up and walk. He used to do a reenactment during our church's worship service, a monologue skit of the lame man miraculously healed by Jesus, who picked up his bed and went off walking and leaping. That was my dad. Prancing around looking ridiculous. His tears would run down his cheeks. That made me ashamed when I was a kid, which was kinda, well, lame. Nobody else would have thought to ridicule him for being ridiculous. There's no dignity in polio, so why should he have any shame in reenacting a healing in Scripture? And he was a method actor— he had experienced his own healing. Now I know, not exactly what it's like to be paralyzed, the torment my father endured when he was a little boy, but at least what it's like to walk with a crutch and have hellfire in my bones from gout. His affliction was more acute, deadly. Mine more long-term. They aren't comparable except that dad and I both know what it's like to be lame and what it's like to be grateful for medicine and healing.

That is why, after 1000 miles, my greatest gratitude is for the simple ability to walk. When I got my trekking poles in the mail and tried them out on the trail, I almost cried. For once I was using a stick to walk because I wanted to, not because I needed to. Thanks to an inexpensive medicine I take every day, I could pursue my desire to walk the Camino. If you are reading this and are not able to walk, in a wheelchair or paralyzed, I believe you can still find a way to travel, to zoom with your feet, even if it is in the mind: that Way is the way of books. Books survive the Lindy effect. Books are old roads, highways to other places and other times, other cultures and other ways of thinking. I am hopeful that people who read of faraway places and times long ago can find some of the same benefits that a Pilgrim finds on the Camino. There is no question in my mind that you can live with purpose and zoom with your feet, because you can be creative about what it means to travel an old road.

I recently heard of a book called *I'll Push You*. It is about two friends who undertook the Camino, one pushing the other in a wheelchair.[8] That's another possibility. That's another Way.

When I was training for the Camino at home, I was always hustling. Timing myself. I had to make sure I was back to the new road in time for my next Zoom call. Training on weekends was better, but there were still obligations to get home for. Supper with the family. A social engagement. A few chores to do before bed. But with no Zoom application calls waiting for me on the Camino, the old road became a way of relaxation. Walking briskly when I wanted or stopping to take photos or get a drink of water, because there was nothing at the end of the road for that day but the camaraderie of swapping stories with Joe or Alberto or Sammy or Jonas, a meal (meat!) and a bed. On the old roads, the only thing pressing me was the coming darkness. After coming in late on my second day, crossing the bridge into Barcelos after sunset, I decreased my expectations so that wouldn't have to be an issue again. If I hadn't done that, I wouldn't have met Fernanda and so many of the others.

Old roads present the invitation to slow down and see what's around you. New roads are insistent—they are designed for us to use them as quickly as possible.

Getting where you're going is overrated. You know what you want, where you want to end up for the day. That's enough. Enjoy the journey! Rome was not built in a day, neither was the Via Romana XIX. The new road takes you to a mall where you spend your money on things you don't need to carry. The new road takes you to places where you spend your energy on things that someone else says should be done by the end of the day, where you take on responsibility for burdens you don't need to bear. The new road takes you to places where you spend your time on things that don't matter, taking on cares that you don't want to carry. The new road makes you forget that clean, dry underwear and meat, (baboon or zebra, anyone?) are all you really need.

On the old road, you only carry what you need, want, and decide to carry.

Old roads, new friends suggests a progression, the former is often needed for the latter to take place. Do not overlook the value of old roads at the beginning of the process, because when we are zipping about on new roads, we rarely keep our eyes open for new friends.

Chapter 2

Bridges

Even the oldest road, the sea, requires a bridge; that is, a boat.

When the Romans first came to the Lima River in what is now northern Portugal, they were terrified of it. They thought it bore a resemblance to the mythical River of Forgetfulness, that is, Lethe, one of the five rivers of the Underworld, and so they believed that if they drank from the river or crossed it, they would lose their memories. Few things are more terrifying than pure amnesia and the oblivion that comes with it. It's one thing to forget everything, and another thing to be forgotten. Imagine losing your memory! How disorienting! Would you not become a wanderer, unsure of who you are, where you came from, unsure also of what you want and where you're going?

In 138 A.D., a campaigning Roman general named Decimus Junius Brutus took his horse across the Lima and turned back to face his troops. In so doing, he showed them: he had not lost his memory. He still recognized his own men. They were commanded to shout their own names as they crossed, to prove even further to themselves that they were not crossing into oblivion as they went.

It strikes me as normal for humans to be far from home and begin to worry that you will forget everything and be forgotten in the face and in the aftermath of your new adventures, paving new roads. But the Romans had nothing to worry about. The Lima is a calm river and contains no magic other than the beauty of water. In the time of Caesar Augustus, when they were paving new roads through Celtic Lusitania and

Galicia, the Romans built Via Romana XIX from Braga, Portugal, north to what is now Santiago, including a bridge at Lima. It continued on from Santiago east toward Lugo and terminated in the city of Astorga in modern-day Spain. Adventures on old roads must include bridges. The bridge creates a focused place to cross over to a far shore, while the two ends of the bridge become natural gathering places where one might find new friends, funneling us toward something that is rather the opposite of the amnesia the Romans feared.

What is the Internet but the newest road, and a bridge across time and space? I have attempted to take my products and services to market over this new bridge, but I find it difficult, slow going, to create new friends on new roads. The Internet is cluttered, as if The Ten Thousand Things were condensed into a can like milk, too sweet, too rich; most people experience this wide new marketplace as a deathtrap of distractions. Even this book itself will be taken to market in this way! Over several months I created a thousand new contacts on LinkedIn, but few of them became friends. In spite of fantastic bridges like personal-interest-matching algorithms used by companies like Lunchclub, we make acquaintances, but we don't often make true friends. I know that often my difficulty in taking my products and services to market is increased by the complexity of who I am that defies algorithms and makes it difficult for people to connect with me. But everyone I meet is complex, too. Algorithms seek to simplify, but the human spirit is indomitable in clinging to pure variety. We, too, are The Ten Thousand Things.

By contrast, the Camino is an old road creating bridges for new friendships, which develop at warp speed, compared with how long it takes to make new friends via the Internet. On an old road you'll have far fewer new acquaintances, especially during the off-season, but the few new acquaintances become old friends overnight, as you cross these ancient bridges together. By some magic of the old road (I know I said it wasn't magical, but in some ways, it is) the old road becomes the bridge to something that might be the opposite of losing one's memory. Something here separates us from the complexity and removes the necessity of matching algorithms for us to connect to new friends. Would an algorithm have connected me with any of the individuals I befriended, even one person on this journey? It is doubtful, with one exception— we now share a common interest in the Camino, and an algorithm might even have brought you, the reader, into contact with Hugo and Sabrina and me because of that single common interest. But while you're on the Camino itself, the matching algorithm is simple. Are you walking the same road, crossing the same bridge at the same time? Who you are, in all your complexity, doesn't matter. You converge upon the same place at the same time, and there you are, and there are your new friends.

A bridge over a river that creates a phenomenon which is the opposite of losing your memory reminds me of the idea of anti-fragility. Nassim Nicholas Taleb described a new concept in his book *Antifragile* which says that the opposite of fragility is not robustness but anti-fragility, meaning something that is not only impervious to shock, but which also increases in strength when subjected to stress. In a similar sort of continuum, there must be a stronger opposite for amnesia than simply the retention of existing memories. Farther along the continuum, we find the making of new memories. I propose that there's another outlying station beyond that, where we find the instantaneous creation of an old memory, which is technically new but has the exact, authentic patina of an old one. Although the memory and friendship are new, it is not artificial, but deep. That is the true opposite of amnesia.

Lost memory <<>> retained memory <<>> creating new memory <<>> instantly creating old memory

How it happens may be a mystery, but as a writer who needs words, like a carpenter needs a hammer and nails to build something, my first puzzle was: What is the word for this?

First there is an experience that creates a memory that has all the rich patina of an old memory. What is this? Is this an experience that connects us with the humanity we've always known in ourselves and others but haven't recognized in a stranger since we were three years old? Or is it a new knowing, just like any other new memory, only crystallized as we cross simple bridges together in such a way as to make that memory an old one overnight? At first, I explored the idea that it is like the downloading of new skills and abilities depicted in The Matrix, as if the characters had always known how to do certain things, not only with their intellect but with the muscle memories required to perform the tasks flawlessly. But that isn't quite adequate. Those new skills are attributed to a download, not an event on an old road, and they implant memories artificially, not authentically. And in those movies the new memories involve skills. They aren't relational, they don't point to friendships that are new-but-old. The event I'm talking about isn't like the Matrix, an Internet-to-brain download.

If the phenomenon is the effect of a cause, then perhaps the important thing to understand is the causal act itself. We may never understand the effect completely, but if we like what we're getting, and we understand the cause, then at least we can acquire the effect repeatedly even if we don't understand the chemistry of it. Kind of like how we don't have to understand electricity to flip the light switch and get what we want.

I had to examine the opposite cause first because it's better understood. The acts that produce amnesia are often traumatic. For example, the multiple mini concussions like American football players and boxers get in pursuit of competitive sport. While few of these register as injuries, over time the repeated traumas cause brain damage which can lead to amnesia and other Parkinson's-like symptoms.

I think that social media and meme culture threatens to do a similar thing to us socially. There is an amnesia of how to converse, how to relate, to build friendships, to create bridges, when social media constantly undermines the footings and pylons of the bridges of friendship.

What is the opposite of this constant mini-bombardment assault upon our memory of how to be human? I call it a *noncussion*. A series of mini-moments, or one large moment, in which we do not have our brains bombarded, instead, our brain is given clear space, which creates a bridge across the river of remembering how to relate and building those relationships with such extreme clarity and focus apart from the normal distractions so that they harden as if they were in a kiln. The metaphor of the bridge is useful because with a boat or strong swimming a river can be crossed at multiple points, but with a bridge there is a focal point for crossing which people without boats and uninterested in swimming can go to, as a detour, yes, but one that provides safe crossing.

Having a noncussion, a time free from bombardment in a place that requires a detour, is a piece of discovering these new-but-old memories and relationships, to developing friends. I remember Roberta telling me that she said to her grumbling walking companion, after knowing one another for a whole day, "In all the time that I've known you, have I ever lied to you?" Not having lied to one another for a full twenty-four hours may be part of the noncussion, in other words, living in pure truthfulness. Be honest with yourself now: the last time you met someone at a party, a blind date, fixed up by friends, or on the Internet, how long did it take you to paint yourself as something you're not? To falsify and make yourself seem just a bit better?

Now, if the opposite of losing memories is not only retaining them but gaining memories with the patina of years on them in a moment, am I describing a place where we connect with what French sociologist Emile Durkheim called the "conscience collective"? Or am I describing a sort of humanistic communion? Am I describing time travel? I like the idea of time travel in the act of slowing down and taking the time to walk along an old road. Most time travel fiction imagines people moving at warp speed to get across the barrier of living in the now to living in the past or future. In the movie Back to the Future, Marty must accelerate the DeLorean to 88 miles per hour, to catch the lightning bolt that propels him into the past.

But perhaps the simplest way to travel through time to earn that new memory with an old patina, that kiln-baked friendship, is not to speed up even more, but to slow down to a walking pace on an old road, find the bridge of memories, and cross over it with someone who is moving at the same, slow speed.

This is my definition of Noncussion: a) the act of crossing the hyper-focusing bridge (detour to a place of common crossing) of old-road time-traveling (walking) and bread-and-wine-sharing communion (eating) together, so that you get the opposite effect of what you get when you're bombarded with mini-concussions on all the speedy roads you normally take. b) A time of traveling where the travel is the end, not just the means to get somewhere else.

My wife is an introvert. She wondered if this kind of thing only happens for extroverts. Most of the folks I talked to were extroverts, so she might be right, but I think some introverts were drawn into the community, too. I had the impression that Jasmine and Sabrina were introverts, but they were with us a lot and clearly enjoyed it. I saw people who went at different speeds, and I don't know if they slowed down enough to get a noncussion; perhaps they were introverts and didn't want to be around other people, but I don't think that's it. It was as if they were treating the Camino like a race, going for the fastest time, trying to beat a personal record or something. I can't judge that as wrong. There are many ways to do the Camino and racing along it as fast as you can is one way to do it. But I suggest that you are less likely to experience a noncussion that way.

As an extreme extrovert, part of my goal was to immerse myself in solitude. I made sure to take time to walk much of the Old Road on my own. In fifteen days walking on the Camino and exploring Santiago and Porto afterward, I had eight days where I walked alone for 90 to 100 percent of the day. Four more days I walked alone for 25 to 50 percent of the day. There were only three days when I walked with other people the entire time. Yet I felt (and others agreed) that I was very sociable. Indeed, I was. If I walked two-thirds of the Camino alone, that accounts for around 47 hours of solitude in 18 days: Not working. Not cooking or driving or writing. Those are hours of solitude, walking. Did I mention that I'm an extreme extrovert? Did I get up in your face yet and say that I'm an EXTREME EXTROVERT? I am no monk. But to my own surprise I did this without ever feeling lonely. I think it was the extensive nature of my training that prepared me for this; I spent many more hours walking alone in 2021 not on the Camino than the hours I spent alone that were on the Camino.

> I am no monk.

It could be that those who don't slow down enough to get a noncussion are missing the point of the Camino. Or maybe, since it is their Camino, they need something other than a noncussion! When I crossed the river into Spain from Portugal, a guy from Juarez caught up to me right in the middle of the bridge. I told him it was ironic that an American and a Mexican could walk north across a river from one country into a different country and nobody would ask either of them to see any papers. The European Union is truly a magnificent beast. Perhaps my European friends would disagree. Anyway, I can imagine a joke starting that way: *"An American, a Mexican, and an Irishman walk across a bridge from Portugal into Spain. The American says..."*

The Mexican guy didn't seem to think it was funny. To be fair, I don't have a punch line yet.

Yes, he said, for him, crossing the border into Texas is truly a hassle. And then he was gone. We met on the bridge, but nothing happened. Maybe he was getting his noncussion a different way. I never saw him again. I forgot his name. Why didn't he walk with me for a while? Was it because I was rude about border crossing? I'm usually able to communicate things like that with a sense of humor. I don't think that was the problem. Remember, I'm the friendliest guy. He was walking faster. Probably wanted to be alone. If I am the friendliest guy, that means there are other guys who are not as friendly. Anyway, I was probably just walking too slowly. I can accept that. One mustn't mind when someone else chooses to pass on by after a short exchange.

A few hours after I returned to Porto, I was chatting with a German guy named Sven, and we came up with these reasons why you might choose not to walk with someone:

1. They are walking too fast or too slow.

2. They are talking too much or too little.

3. They are not comfortable enough to walk on their own, and act as if they need you.

4. And the most obvious reason, so obvious indeed that Sven and I didn't mention it to each other:

5. You want to be alone.

It has nothing to do with the other person. Whether you like them or not, whether they fit any of the indicators above or not, it is legitimate to walk alone just because that's what you want. And it is legitimate for someone else to do the same. We have to be comfortable walking alone, and so does the other person, to make these bridges work.

We have to be able to recognize that *sonder* is always at work. Sonder, an idea from the *Dictionary of Obscure Sorrows*, is the realization that each random passerby is living a life as vivid and complex as your own… in which you might appear only once as an extra, sipping coffee in the background… To notice moments of sonder in the passing of strangers requires a strong Theory of Mind (empathy).

My Camino friends are Pilgrims-never-met to someone like my friend Jonathan, who did a different route in a different month. For that matter, I am that passerby to dozens of people who walked a different route and arrived in front of the Cathedral in Santiago within the same half-hour.

So, the stars align on these bridges. Or they don't, and that's okay too. We take the old road, find the bridge over the river, have a noncussion experience alone, or together, and something happens. Then, if we choose to walk at the same pace and talk and listen in relatively equal shares, and we are both comfortable walking on our own, if we choose to enjoy a meal together, if we chat while sitting on bunks in an albergue, the magic of the bridge can come into effect.

I gave a word to the causal event, then found myself with a definition for the effect but no word for the definition: 1) The mental and social effect that is caused by a noncussion on the old road, an event bridging the gaps between two people so that they co-create a new-yet-rich-with-patina relational memory, or, 2) that memory itself.

What to call this thing? I worked forward from concussion to define the causal activity as a *noncussion*, but now must work backward to find a name for the effect. 'Amnesia' comes from the Greek *amnesi*, the prefix "*a-*" meaning "not" and *mnesi*, which is related to mindfulness, thinking. The Greeks had a word called *amnestia* which had to do with the forgetting of wrongs and is also related to the English word *amnesty* and the concept of sheltering and forgiveness. Next, I toyed around with an interesting English play on Greek words, which came to my mind from the suffix *-nesia*, meaning "islands" (as in Polynesia) from the Greek *nesos*. True to John Donne's "No man is an island" poem, we recognize the need for experiencing the noncussions to keep us connected in this way to what the poet called "Europe," and "the maine," rather than isolated. John

Donne was letting us know that he recognizes sonder, but he says we are not excused from caring about humanity simply because of our unfamiliarity with the complexity of the life of another human being... which has expired when the bell tolls. Their death is our loss, too.

The bell tolls for you.

The noncussion event connects us via a magical bridge to other islands (humans), so that we connect with the whole of humanity.

Inspired by *Ponte*, which is the Galician and Portuguese word for "bridge", I submit that *pontenesia* is an appropriate appellation for the phenomena. So noncussion is the cause, and pontenesia is the effect of noncussions. In other words, the new-but-authentically-old friendship and, secondly, that new-old memory of friendship itself.

We need these, because, as John Donne noted, otherwise, we are all just a bunch of "clods".

Imagine a deserted island. You can do this because it is a popular cartoon trope. The island is about five meters wide and has one palm tree. You have grown a beard. (Why are the ma-

> We are all clods.

rooned suckers in the cartoons always men? Answer: because the man's beard is a convenient convention for showing how long the sucker has been marooned.) Perhaps you were invited to bring one item ashore; imagine a book or a bottle of water ... whatever it was, you probably chose the wrong item. The island can be a hell, either because you are alone (like *Robinson Crusoe* or Tom Hanks' character in *Castaway*) or because you are there with a psychopath and some cult-followers (*Lord of the Flies*) or it can be a paradise, at least initially, because your oldest and best friend or your lover is there, or because, in the moment you got stranded, someone else did too, and they're companionable and you get on well enough, and you support one another, give one another space, and have no worries.

This island could be you and your social media presence. The island could be you and your incessant wandering, unsure of what you want. Ultimately you will need real bridges to other islands. Even being with your best friend and lover will go wrong if they are the only person you ever spend time with. You need to find a place to get your noncussions, because from time to time you need to experience pontenesia, finding new friends who seem as if you've always known them after one day's hike.

New friends cross over this magical bridge on the Camino to the far bank where the friendship of a few hours feels like the friendship of deepest memories, as if we had known each other from childhood, as if our mothers had been part of the sisterhood of a small village, as if our grandmothers had been cousins. This anti-amnesia is not a download but a true memory, connecting a recent transaction to the old business of being human in a way that catalyzes a chemical reaction which creates the patina of decades of friendship into just a few miles of walking together.

How do I know it's a real thing? That it's not just me? I asked others about their experiences. I met Roberta after it was all over. Roberta's story confirms the concept. She told me that she was walking with an 80-year-old companion for a day or two, until they felt like old friends. When he was awash in some complaint or anxiety, she attempted to encourage him, and when he persisted in negativity, she responded, "In all the time I've known you, have I ever lied to you?" The patina of old friendship was already there. I debriefed with Jonathan about this, and he also affirmed the idea. It's not just something that happened to me. It happens to many people on the Camino.

There is a bridge across the Lima River at the aptly named city of Ponte de Lima. It was rebuilt or restored in 1368, mostly on top of the remains of the Roman foundations; five of the existing arches were built 2000 years ago by the Romans. Of all the ancient bridges I saw on the Via Romana XIX I think the Ponte de Lima is the most beautiful. In the evening, I was hanging out with Sammy on the north bank of The Lima. I tried to jump up on the statue to sit on the horse behind General Decimus Junius Brutus for a picture. Sammy took my picture as I slipped off the horse's leg and fell with a splat on my rear in the mud. Shocked, she first made sure I was okay. Laughing, I said, "I'm fine, keep taking pictures!" Trying to mount up behind the General was the dumbest thing I did on the entire trip. I am a child, I am clod. I am an island, but the

Ponte de Lima was a great place for a noncussion.

And now, thanks to pontenesia... Sammy and I have been new friends forever.

> **I fell with a splat on my rear.**

I said, to Sammy, toward the end of a long day from Ponte de Lima to Rubiães, that I thought the Camino would be a great way for two people to find out if they're right for each other before getting married. Not to have some sort of romantic getaway, not for making love or even for being alone together, but for the opportunity to see how the other person deals with adversity, for how they handle you, too, when it is not going well– for how they interact with people they've just met, how they present themselves. (Is it done honestly? Or with some false braggadocio?) Sammy turned to me in shock and said, "look at my arm!" Her hair was standing on end. She had been thinking the same idea exactly.

The Camino is raw, a place where truth prevails. It will reveal whether or not you're able to be a good friend. A solid companion. Strong enough to be alone, friendly enough to be together, wise enough to know which is appropriate in the moment. Next, we begin to explore what we can do to prepare to be a good friend.

Chapter 3

Travelers and Thieves

There is no calamity like not knowing what is enough. - Lao Tzu[9]

The Civilized and the Barbarians.

Jews and Gentiles.

Saints and Sinners.

Faithful and Infidel.

The Enlightened and the Unenlightened.

The Woke and the Canceled.

The Carbon Neutral-Footprint and the Carbon-Emitting.

Our human condition is more complex than all the binary options we are normally presented, each one a bounded-set model.[10]

For a long time, we've had terminology to describe ourselves as In and others as Out. We use our measuring tools to determine who is out and spend the dregs of our emotional energy on the hope that others will find that we also deserve to remain on the inside. Do we deserve a seat at the table? Therein lies the problem.

We judge others rather than concerning ourselves first with ourselves. *Do not judge, or you too will be judged*.[11] If only we could do that. But we can't. We really struggle not to place ourselves and others into camps or tribes. To measure one another and find each other satisfactory or lacking. One huge problem is the measuring tools themselves. The tools don't measure up. The tools society gives us for assessing others are designed for bounded-set thinking. I propose instead a heuristic for centered-set thinking, which describes people's orientation as "headed toward" or "headed away from" a certain point and is much more inclusive.

Even the nature of being male and female is bounded set. I had a long conversation at Fernanda's with the pilgrims from Finland who are non-binary. I made the mistake of placing them in the camp of "women" or "girls". They corrected me, gently but firmly. We had a long discussion about assumptions; even the Finns had to agree that they also assumed that I was a man. It happens. We all do it. We cannot walk through every day questioning all the Ten Thousand Things, both the obvious ones and those that seem obvious and aren't. Whatever else they may or may not be, Maya and Esse are human. They deserve a welcome seat at the table. They, too, are travelers.

Male, Female, non-binary. American, Egyptian, dual citizen.

The Righteous, the Unrighteous, and the Self-Righteous.

Creator, Child, Spirit of Family, and the Universe.

The One, the Two, the Three, and the Ten Thouxings of the Tao.

The reality is that we're all Travelers, who are at times Wanderers and/or Thieves. So, the heuristic (rule of thumb) is to ask oneself:

Do I know what I want and need, and where I'm going? Am I wandering?

Am I taking more than my share? Am I willing to give when I can? Am I willing to receive? Am I a thief right now?

The assumption to carry about others is this: whatever else they may be, that other person is a pilgrim, a traveler. They deserve a seat at the table, the respect of conversation, the opportunity to become our friend. Can I reserve judgment long enough to allow that friendship to happen?

Imagine the pilgrim of days gone by; in times when that pilgrim's journey isn't complete at Santiago, because there is no bus, train or airplane to carry them back to Porto or St. Jean or wherever they came from; rather, they must not only journey to Santiago, but they must also then turn around and walk home. St. Francis of Assisi was one of these pilgrims in the 1200s. It took him several years to go to Santiago and to return home. What challenges did they face that we do not? Perhaps the way wasn't marked, and they got lost. Perhaps they found a man with a cart full of straw who was moving in the right direction, and they accepted a ride. (Now, hitching a ride seems to most pilgrims like cheating. I'm sure for the pilgrim of yesterday that would be considered a smart way of saving precious energy. Remember, meat was much less likely to be served in the time of St. Francis's pilgrimage.) Perhaps they came to a river and had to follow it east to find the bridge. Perhaps they were easily able to follow the Via Romana XIX. They had no reliable map, or for that matter, no reliable app or GPS. In any case, if they were not wealthy, they may have had to accept the help of hundreds of strangers to make it to Santiago and back. There were people who respected the sacred nature of the journey enough to offer them a roof, a meal, a drink of water. Perhaps those people thought that they would also receive a blessing just for helping— if they believed so, then they did. The traveler may have accepted the welcome and the simple food and silence of the monks at a monastery.

Sometimes the traveler had to take what they needed from the environment. Even as we do today, the pilgrims took an orange or two from a tree overhanging the path. Or some chestnuts or apples. Jonathan told me he saw no orange trees on the Camino Primitivo, it's too far north. But he found a tree full of ripe plums in a field. Free for the taking. One toss of a rock into the tree, and dozens of plums fell. He picked up a dozen. We laughed at the idea of him filling his entire pack with them. More than he needs. Hundreds. He could have done it and done harm to nobody else. But what would be the point? If he ate them all, he'd get sick. If he didn't, they'd rot in his pack. And in any case, he'd have to carry all that weight. What else could he do with such treasure? Bury those plums in a hole as if they were pirate's rubies? He was walking alone but even if he'd had five friends there was no need to take all the plums from the tree. There were so many reasons why it was laughable, preposterous, to take more than what he needed for the day. He gathered what manna he needed and went on. So often, aren't we trying to figure out how to sweep all of the plums into our pack to keep for ourselves?

The confident traveler takes only what he or she needs. This is an easy rule to abide by, when you must carry everything you take on your back. If you have extra food, you can leave it at the albergue and someone else can eat it. There's no point in wasting anything. Share what you have, and graciously accept anything that is given to you with no expectation of payment. But sometimes we are afraid. We are afraid that there will be no gift for us as a traveler. We are afraid that our provisions will be empty, or water will run dry. So we take on more than we need, more than we can truly carry. This is a metaphor for spiritual life. We often take up burdens that are too heavy, instead of fruit, which is light. When we take something more than we need to our own detriment, the weight will not only be too much for us, but it can extend to the injury of others around us. We don't know what is enough, so we cause injury to ourselves and others by trying to carry too much, and that is the calamity Lao Tzu is talking about.

By contrast, Jesus said *my burden is light*. When I visited Hopkins, Belize in February 2022, I spoke with a friend of mine named Pastor Hurdie, who said, "If you're burned out, it probably means you're doing something wrong." Taking on too much. Assuming you're the one who has to carry something that you have no business carrying.

For many people, even those traveling to Santiago to visit the remains of Saint James, the older measuring sticks may feel clumsy and disorienting, like when someone says the temperature is seven degrees outdoors (meaning Celsius) and my mind is used to Fahrenheit. Even for Christians whose holy book includes the terminology of saint and sinner as in/out measuring stick, we are culturally at a place where the saint/sinner dichotomous language has become disorienting and largely passe. And anyway, a careful reading of Scripture would indicate that so long as we live, while we are saints, we are still also sinners, and while we are sinners we can also be saints. This isn't an excuse for bad behavior, it's just that these words too easily become thought-ending statements. They don't require us to ask ourselves these questions and use the heuristics, rules of thumb, to determine how we are oriented. For a centered-set way of thinking is all about orientation and direction.

While I accept these words, saint and sinner, as one accurate depiction of reality, I recognize that some new measuring sticks, new language, might help us to be oriented in today's world. What is a sin in the postmodern world, where we say that whatever feels good is fair game? Take as much as you like! Perhaps a sin is now defined as "anything that might cause you to be canceled." How do I judge myself, saint or sinner, considering the issue of how to do so without falling into that abhorrent camp of the self-righteous, the judges and cancelers? Perhaps, while we in the Christian tradition rely on grace for our iniquities (calamities caused) all of us, Christian or atheist, Buddhist, or Muslim, could still examine ourselves in this way:

I am a traveler, every day. Sometimes I take just enough. Sometimes more than enough. Do I even know what is enough? Am I wandering? And if I don't know what enough is, then how can I be sure that today I am not also a thief, as I travel or wander? To answer the questions posed by these heuristics will require what modern psychology calls *agency*: the ability to accurately identify and assess one's own situation and ability to change. This makes it possible for us to take a good hard look at what is enough.

I propose a new measuring tool, one where we all start out as human, allowing ourselves an automatic seat at the table as an insider, and we begin by taking what we need to fulfill the role of human. We are all Travelers, and we accept that this means we have both needs and desires. We may earn our keep, but there will be other times when we are given gifts. A traveler earns what she can, gracefully accepts any gifts, for if it is better to give than to receive, why would she rob someone else of that blessing? Even refusing a gift could be thievery.

For the physical traveler or wanderer, the needs are simple. Food. Drink. A warm, dry place to sleep. Getting our desires in focus is always more difficult. The traveler must take these things which are needed to be able to continue the next day. For very early pilgrims who were not nobles, it must have been a regularly humbling event to receive from others what was needed to continue. A meal, a place to sleep, even the simple assistance of letting you know you're no longer on your way and need to turn back. Once, when I was chatting away with Hugo as we walked, someone pulled her car up and stopped us. We had missed an arrow and had to turn back, perhaps fifty meters. Thank God it wasn't more! How did she know we were off track? A few minutes later, back on track ourselves, we saw this same woman get out of her car and go into her house. She lived on the street in her town that was the Camino itself.

One can hardly imagine a pilgrim on a spiritual quest who takes things without asking, but in fact it wasn't uncommon to find an apple or orange hanging on a tree over the wall into the public space and pluck it. Whatever is in the common space is free for taking. If you're hungry, take it. But if you're afraid of going hungry, you're tempted to take more than you need. I never took twenty oranges just to allow them to rot in my bag! It would be too heavy! What weighs on your back also weighs on your soul. Or is it the other way around?

Could a pilgrim ever be a thief? Of course. A pilgrim is just a traveler and a human, with all the potential to be afraid, and the potential to react by grabbing too much. A person I knew from my hometown who made the pilgrimage to Santiago a decade ago had his very boots stolen on the Camino. Was it a pilgrim? Who knows? But it was a traveler of some kind who did this thievery.

I met this amusing young guy from Poland; he might be the same age as my oldest son. His sneakers were shot. I don't know why he kept them. He was wearing sandals with weird extra padding under his feet; he insisted that what he was wearing on his feet was "the best". I was approaching an albergue and The Kid was leaving; there was no host at the albergue, he said, so he had already decided to go to the next town! It was two in the afternoon and there were 15 more miles to reach it! After he moved on, I sent Alberto a message, suggesting he watch out for The Kid. I figured

𝔉eminine 𝔥𝔶giene pads make comfy cushions for blistered feet.

he'd be getting to Vilanova de Arousa late in the evening. But just two hours later Alberto replied that the Polish Kid had already arrived. It turned out that he had hitchhiked when it got late in the day. Some might say it was cheating. People have opinions about how the Camino ought to be done, but I say he was doing things his own way, making it his Camino. Alberto also confirmed what I suspected about the Kid's strangely padded footwear: The Kid had discovered that feminine hygiene pads were comfy cushions for his blisters. I suppose they also did a great job soaking up sweat

At least he did not steal someone's boots. He determined what was enough: the feminine hygiene pads were enough, and that deserves respect even though I'm still laughing about it. Not being a thief sometimes requires creative solutions! I didn't meet anyone whom I thought would steal anything nearly as important as a pair of boots from another traveler, but I always kept my passport and my money close. You never know when fear will strike in the heart of another Traveler, but you can be sure that sooner or later, it will catch up with someone, and for a moment while your wallet is unguarded the other traveler loses sight of Enough and while he or she is still a traveler, in that moment they could also become a thief.

Still, the one thing that I took along and never used was a small lock to put on a locker. It was advised in various blogs, but I never found a locker in an albergue that required me to use my own lock and key; I suppose those are more common on the French Camino. On the Portuguese route, rarely was there even a locker of any kind. While it is prudent to keep close tabs on your most valuable items so others don't take it in a moment of weakness, what is even more important is to consider for ourselves what we need, and what might be more than what we need.

The calamity of thieving, like taking extra oranges or plums, is a weight upon our own shoulders and must be avoided! If I eat more food than I need, just 100 calories a day, over time I gain weight. I have not recognized what is enough, and I have added weight to my own shoulders... and hips, knees and ankles. If I keep more money than what I need, I add weight to my soul.

The famous writer John Wesley, whose writing earned £30,000 in his lifetime, lived during a time when a man could live on £30 for a year. But despite the wealth his creative work generated, Wesley ended his life with nothing but pocket change, saying, "When I die if I leave behind me ten pounds ... you and all mankind can bear witness against me that I have lived and died a thief and a robber." [12] Wesley figured out what was enough and lived on that. He was vigilant against his own thievery.

For as long as we have been human, we have been traveling and taking things from the environment as we go, receiving gifts from those who support us along the way. Those who would have us work towards carbon-neutrality find themselves aghast as people continue to fly here and there, burning and burning jet fuel. One of my friends on the Camino, one of the fine folks from Finland, said that they didn't know if they would ever do it again because it required air travel to arrive at the starting point. At first, I thought that was a bit ridiculous (how easy it is to scoff at this, or at people who have chosen to wear feminine hygiene products as foot cushions, or any limitation on Enough that someone else has decided for themselves). But perhaps they are right: for them, one Camino is enough, two is thievery. At least that person is conscious of what they are taking and what they really need. For me, I think one Camino is not enough and I'll have to fly again.

Rule of thumb: don't be in a hurry to judge other peoples' 'Enough' but know your own.

When it comes to carbon footprint, it's so hard to say how much a flight to Porto costs. There are myriad calculations: the cost of building airports and manufacturing airplanes, driving to and from the airport, the plastic waste of prepackaged airline meals; the list of offenses against the environment go on and on when we fly. The problem with trying to convince other humans not to fly is the problem of trying to convince humans not to be humans, for at a basic level we are travelers; we have craved flight since long before the Greeks told tales of Icharus flying too close to the sun and melting his wings. Perhaps I have strayed into the territory of the self-righteous already because I am justifying the flight plans for all of us who simply wish to fly or travel.

Traveling always has a cost. Even animals who travel require additional calories.

It's not like we can hibernate, and if we could we'd have to consume extra to make it through the long winter. Does a bear know what is enough when she gorges herself in October? But I simply do not believe, now that we have learned to fly, that we are likely to discontinue the practice entirely. Technology that allows a human the ability to fly is a new road, to be sure, and has only been widely available for a hundred years or so. I don't know if any of my great-grandfathers and great-grandmothers ever took a ride in an airplane. According to the Lindy effect it may only be with us for another hundred years. But I doubt that. When you look at the Lindy effect from the perspective of how long people have had the desire to fly, it would indicate much more clearly that we're never going to stop. Perhaps it is to our imminent demise. Perhaps the Greek tale of Icharus was a warning parable for us; a story of humanity's uncheckable hubris. We are stealing something: taking more than necessary. We are prone to this and rarely ask ourselves what is enough. The cost is there. Unmistakable. But on the other hand: Just as difficult to calculate as the cost of flying to Porto from Finland or Indiana is the cost of a world where nobody travels. What is the cost of isolation?

Without travel, no noncussions.

Perhaps what is freshest in everyone's mind is the isolation we experienced during the Covid pandemic. We only got a bombardment of anxious thoughts, mini concussions, as we scrolled Facebook wondering if this was the end of the world as we know it. "I feel fine," I said to myself, even as I canceled plans to visit Barcelona in 2020. I felt the panic building.

I remember reading a humorous book as a kid called *A Fine and Pleasant Misery* by the late outdoors magazine writer Pat McManus, who was an expert on getting lost in the woods and panicking. *"First of all, one is either a panicker or one isn't, and the occasion of being lost is no time to start fretting about a flaw in one's character. My own theory holds that it is best, if one is a panicker, to get the panic out of the system as quickly as possible."*[13] Pat detailed a variety of methods for panic people could deploy when lost in the woods, which, as I recall, included a sort of mobile panic where you sprint through nature bouncing off trees and boulders, as well as several versions of the stationary panic, where you freaked out while not going anywhere. Bombardment leads to panic. The pandemic was democratic in its opportunity for stationary panic. We all sat in our flats and apartments and villas and houses and yurts and panicked in place.

"I feel fine," I said again, once I had gotten the panic out of my system, that stationary panicking in my flat in Cairo which lasted for a few weeks, after which Megan and I moved our family home. That's about the time I started walking regularly; 18 months before I hiked the Camino.

Without noncussions, no pontenesia.
Without pontenesia, no new friends.

In the 1980s we had perspectives about the Russians, the Soviets, that were born of isolation. We didn't know any Russians! As much as we need to not fly to protect our earth from carbon emissions, we also need to travel somehow, to see how people live, or we'll find ourselves isolated and insulated against other tribes and cultures, locked into one way of thinking. We can't live together on this planet without finding new friends from time to time, friends from a thousand different backgrounds, new friends whose social positions we can't accurately guess as poor or rich; whose genders we can't accurately identify as male or female. That friend from Finland? I thought they were 'she', but I was gently corrected. They and their companion became friends who challenged my bounded-set assumptions.

What wars are avoided when we travel and meet other Travelers and sit for a meal together? When we meet Wanderers and offer a bit of encouragement? When we meet adversity and choose not to be Theives? Who can say what terrible destruction is averted?

The difference between being a traveler and a thief is nuanced territory, a gray area where each of us must make his or her own decision about what is enough, always knowing that because of the limits of our agency and clarity of thought about this issue, we may be wrong. There are easy calculations: do you take someone's boots or cash without asking? No!

And there are complicated ones: do you fly to Porto to walk for three weeks? Hard to say. Did I take more than what was enough already? Would going a second time be taking too much?

It is not until we traveled that we began to encounter the Other People and begin to brand them as the Barbarians. Perhaps our warring began when we went in search of fresh water or food. On the other hand, it isn't until we traveled that we began sharing ideas, technology, even religion. I remember talking with Samuel in Ivory Coast when I was a college student. "Isn't it horrible how the Europeans came here and forced their culture and religion on you?" one of my fellow students asked. Our cultural guide, Samuel Zaki, who knew better than most of the American students how much the European colonists had taken from his homeland, replied, "Yes, but if they hadn't, we wouldn't know Jesus."

So, wars have started because our tribes banged into other tribes. And they have ceased because we've taken the time to travel, and sat down to listen to one another, too. And we have shared Jesus and offered stories of other peacemakers as well.

Now, we are Travelers. And we are Thieves. We can ask ourselves the questions. But we don't need to brand others that way any longer— "Barbarian!" We don't need to make war on our neighbors. The new traveler mindset is one of Enough. There is and will be enough for me, and for all the other travelers and wanderers.

One hiker said that he had a rest day built in but wasn't planning to use it unless he had an injury. So long as he felt good, he felt he should keep going, preserving the extra day in the schedule for emergencies. But when he arrived in Santiago, not having used this available rest and trusted that it would help prevent the injuries, he texted me to say: "Just arrived- I'm really f&)@ed- I would have benefited greatly from a rest day. Even the Big Guy who inspired all this pilgrimage lark rested on the 7th." While this traveler achieved the destination, I'm sure he was feeling the burn for a while. By not taking a rest day, he stole from his future self.

Acknowledging *Enough* for each day includes how far to go, and how much to rest.

How easily I could have made the same mistake! I took that rest day in Ponteve-dra even though I felt that I could have moved on. There was a minor strain in my right quad suffered from the steep descent into Redondela. Not a pulled muscle, exactly, but a bit too sore. Did I really have to rest? No, I could have kept going and probably would have been okay. I was over-prepared. Really fit. But yes, I did really have to rest. I had to recognize what was enough. I rested on principle. And I'm so glad I did! I ended up with a beautiful day of sightseeing, enjoyed an incredible free museum with a special origami exhibit and had some great community experience with others who also took a rest day in Pontevedra, eating roasted chestnuts, laughing, and so on. For me, the next four days to Santiago were a joyful experience, even the 35 km (22.8 mile) day from Vilanova de Arousa to Padrón. I arrived without blisters, sore legs, nor strained muscles. I could have walked another 20 miles the day after arriving in Santiago if I had needed to. This story could come across as self-righteous! To be fair it could have easily been my lot to push on when doing so was dangerous. It only so happens that I was the one who chose the restful path in this instance. Just because I knew what enough was and paid attention to it in that moment, I'm not claiming to be a ... saint.

One evening, after everyone had already enjoyed wine with dinner as you do in Europe, the waiter offered a variety of liquors after the meal. One was as green as a witches' brew— there was a witch on the label! I decided I had had enough alcohol and politely declined while the other five Pilgrims each downed a shot. I am not interested in bounded-set thinking that says one should never drink (unless you are in recovery, of course) but prefer to think in terms of what is enough. I struggle a lot more with recog-nizing what is enough when it comes to food! I sure like to eat! It was a pleasure to burn so many calories that I could eat whatever I wanted on the Camino and still lose weight, but that doesn't mean that I didn't occasionally take more than what I needed. We all stop too late sometimes when it comes to taking and receiving.

Avoiding the calamity by knowing what is enough requires us to stop before we're spent. with exercise, sometimes we push ourselves to injury. With food, we eat until our gut hurts. Knowing what is enough with sex, with alcohol— with potentially addictive behaviors and codependency of any sort.

There is one thing that we can take without worrying about theft: we can take our time.

We have to trust that we have been, and will be, given enough of it. Even if we fear that we will not be given enough time, there is no way for us to steal more of it.

We do battle with our thieving nature. Bilbo Baggins, the famous Tolkien character, is a celebrated traveler-turned-thief. Bilbo's biggest challenge was to give up what he'd stolen when the time came for his nephew to discard the Ring. After Tolkien's example, the fantasy literature genre began including Thief as a common archetypal skill, along with such notable archetypal skills as wizard and warrior for the archetypal various races like human, dwarf, elf, giant, and barbarian to employ. Of course, Bilbo is thought of as a good thief. Like Robin Hood, he wasn't about stealing more than enough, but about stealing so others wouldn't go hungry and still others wouldn't retain more than enough power. The Hobbits, a race that was not particularly known for traveling, also had a built-in defense mechanism against the hubris of men (a convenient literary trick), so that Bilbo was able to fulfill his calling as a thief who didn't keep his stolen goods for his own use or power. But we are not Hobbits. And when I am talking about thievery, I'm not talking about being a Robin Hood, or The Professor from the Netflix hit series *Money Heist (Casa de Papel)*.

We are human: We are travelers, and we are thieves. We create our own calamity when we do not recognize what is enough and refuse to take that which we need.

Some Principles

Try to know what is enough. Accept that you will not be perfect at this calculation.

Learn to accept gifts.

Stop before you've spent everything, all your energy, all your cash, or you'll steal from your future self.

Take your time. It is yours. You will have enough of it, and you couldn't steal more if you wanted to.

In all other things, take only what you need. Otherwise, you will be carrying a needless burden, which will only hurt you first.

Travel, or don't, based on your own convictions about what is enough.

| Travel. Or don't. |

Chapter 4

Burdens

I began to think about burdens before I even left for the Camino. In training, I was carefully trying to estimate and guess what items I really needed and packing them along for training hikes. It occurred to me toward the end of a long twelve-mile hike that many people carry burdens they don't need to carry only because they have become comfortable with them. My backpack had become comfortable. It was heavy, to be sure, but I had grown accustomed to carrying it. I could walk five kilometers in an hour with or without the pack, although a long day was more tiring with it. We get used to burdens when we've taken more than we needed and carried it with us long enough. But that doesn't mean they aren't burdens.

Carrying too much weight on your stomach or hips? Fight back.

When it comes to backpacks, with the click of two buckles we could let those things drop and walk away from them, and yet we seem to think we need these burdens we carry. Somehow, they will be useful. Whatever burden you may be hoarding - psychological or physical - you don't need it. With some of our burdens it's as simple as deciding. You can unclip it like the belt on a hiking backpack, and let it crash to the ground.

Then there are the good burdens. I carry a burden. It is a light one for me. It is the vision burning inside my bones, that everyone ought to have one good friend who can walk beside them, not judging them, supporting them, encouraging them. Holding them to their commitments with a good-natured smile. That is why I became a leadership coach. And a second burden, which is related to the first: as much as we commit to action, try to make things happen, work hard, and set goals, life is still absurd. There are ways that I walk a tightrope over a chasm from one side, the seriousness of life, to the other side, the seriousness of death, and in between, filling the void, is the absurdity of it all. And that is why I became a novelist: because everyone who sees this absurdity also needs one good friend walking that tightrope over the chasm of the absurd with them. Why so serious if life is absurd? Because life is also beautiful, and I take beauty seriously. I realized something about myself as a writer during the Camino:

I write my books upon the fine line
Between the absurd and the sublime.

Sometimes I walk that fine line like an acrobat, other times I trip over the line and land on my face like a clown. I'm okay with either result. You can't take risks if you're afraid of looking like a fool.

Either way, whether life is absurd, and death is serious, or the other way around, we all deserve having at least one good friend. We need it, we want it. Finding friendship is a human drive. It's a terrifying prospect to consider that we might take a risk and find ourselves rejected. But friendship is also a thing for which we have great capacity if we prepare ourselves to walk it through and steel ourselves against the prospect of loss.

This burden I carry for friendship must have been given to me by a higher source, because I have found it is not too difficult for me to think about, write about, pray about, and do. It comes naturally to me. I know that it doesn't come naturally to others, which is why I hope to help my readers discover their own capacity for friendship. Jesus said that if we come to him, our burden would be light. Indeed, this is a burden I am happy to carry. I will never drop it like a backpack beside the road. I am always ready to carry the burden of friendship. I am comfortable with the pack on my shoulders, and I don't take it too seriously, either. But I won't unbuckle it and let it fall.

I realized that when Alfonso and Debee gifted me a bottle of wine and I had to carry it to share with my friends in Santiago some 45 miles away, the extra weight ceased being a problem. As soon as I thought of it as a gift to share with my friends, it became a joy.

> A burden that is a gift for friends is a joy.

We can carry things for ourselves and find that the reason we took them along in the first place is to give them away. In a sense, the idea that they will be useful at some point is worth carrying so long as we're confident they'll be useful to someone else! When I met Roberta, she was in a lot of pain. I could see that her knee was badly swollen, it looked like there was a small watermelon in the leg of her pants where the knee should be. I had come to the end of my road, and so had she, but Roberta was nearly immobile in her bed in that albergue in Santiago. How would she get back downstairs for food? How would she get to the airport and get home to Iowa? I didn't know, and I realized those weren't my problems to solve, but I did have something in my pack that would come in handy. I gave her a little plastic baggie containing about 20 tablets of Tylenol. A month later I got a Christmas card from Roberta, hoping that she had located the correct Adam Fleming in searching for my address, and thanking me for the Tylenol. She said that I had no idea how much help it was. She was right. I still don't, although I appreciated the note. In that case, I was giving something I really didn't need any more. Why not let go of something you no longer need and give it to someone who can use it? What better reason to carry a burden in the first place?

Chapter 5

Taking Care of Your Feet

W hat makes someone a friend? As a business owner who has a high value for friendship, I often find that I mesh best with clients who are also interested in having a friendly relationship. To be sure, the relationship with my clients is transactional which may seem to be an odd way of having a friendship. On the other hand, all relationships are transactional in some way.

If one is Thieving, one does not make a good friend.

If one is Wandering, the other person may need to make sacrifices for a friendship to prosper. We'll get into sacrifices a bit more later.

The first thing someone has to do when preparing to be a good friend is taking care of their own feet.

Alberto told me his mother had made the pilgrimage to Fatima. She was a serious Catholic and believed that every blister you got correlated to some sin in your life. "She got a lot of blisters on that first pilgrimage," Alberto said, laughing. Alberto doesn't really believe in such things, or at least he says he doesn't. "After the pilgrimage she started going to church more often!" Alberto may not have been a believer, but he was on the Camino because of a vow. His wife had recently gone through a difficult pregnancy and during that time, he promised (to someone or something) that if the baby was healthy, he would do the Camino in the next year. The baby was healthy. I told Alberto I respected that he was keeping his vow. Alberto admitted to me that since he anticipated a lot of rain, he bought new waterproof boots right before the trip. He didn't take time to break them in. I thought to myself, "Ouch. That's going to hurt." Sure enough, after Alberto made it to Santiago and then returned to his home in Lisbon, he messaged me: "I'm home, my right foot is kaput. Tomorrow I'll go to the hospital to make an X-ray and ask a nurse to take care of the bubbles [blisters]. I got one bloody one that is pretty nasty"

I messaged back: Sorry about your foot. Take care. And remember. Every blister is a sin... ha-ha.

Alberto replied: "Hahaha. That was a huge one! Hope it was forgiven"

I told him I believed it was.

Alberto may not believe in blisters the way his mother does—I mean, as indicators of specific sins we have committed—for he knows on a practical level that blisters are a natural result of not having trained, not having broken in your equipment, and not having taken care of your feet adequately in a number of ways. Blisters are an impracticality and ought to be prevented at all costs! But really a lot of what we call sin comes from not taking care of the basics, making sure to prepare ourselves, toughen up, break in our gear. In fact, the blisters = *sin* metaphor isn't a bad one at all!

I wondered if, subconsciously, Alberto wanted to fulfill his vow with some sort of pain, so that he would know that he had somehow repaid the universe for the healthy birth of his child. Why torture yourself with new boots? Why not do some preparation, break in your shoes? Even if you did prepare, blisters are still always a possibility when you go out to walk fourteen miles in a single day on rough surfaces and across difficult terrain. No amount of preparation is failsafe.

Taking care of your feet is a great metaphor for taking care of yourself spiritually, mentally and emotionally. Nothing will cause us more pain every step of the way than a blister, and nothing will cause you more pain on a daily basis than having something out of order in your spiritual life. There are ways to train oneself spiritually. If we believe ourselves to be on a grand spiritual journey, then why would we not train for this, so that we can continue the journey without suffering or causing unnecessary pain? By training ourselves, we protect ourselves, and we protect others around us from the harm that comes to them when we are not careful, our spiritual feet toughened. St. Paul's direction for taking care of your feet, in his letter to the church at Ephesus, was to put on shoes that are the preparation [readiness] of the good news of peace. I never really noticed the word preparation before. If peace is good news, you've got to break in your shoes, or you're going to walk around talking about peace with blisters on your toes— it would be ironic to talk about peace without experiencing it for yourself!

Shoes have to have grip. More than simply avoiding blisters, good shoes also keep you from slipping, rolling your ankle. But you can't just go on a long march without breaking those shoes in first. Getting and training in good shoes is good preparation. I knew that if I got a serious sprain on the Camino it was over. Once or twice I nearly did it, too. On some stones just outside of Valença, not long before I almost got shot by some game-bird hunter (that's another story), I felt my ankle begin to roll. In Santiago, Jonas ran into some others he had walked with for a time and noticed that one friend wasn't with them. They told him she sprained an ankle very badly and had to quit. If blisters are pain at every step, a sprain is no more steps at all. Sometimes things knock you out of the pilgrimage, and there's not much one can do.

Either way, our shoes are critical equipment that must be part of our preparation. If we take care of our own feet, we can be more cheerful, more pleasant, fuller of good news and peace. We can be a good walking companion. We are ready to be a friend if we are well shod and not worried about our own footing.

In practical terms on the Camino, you may swear off social media for a time, you may do everything possible to avoid the mini-concussions of daily life, but I don't think having that noncussion event and crossing the bridge to a pontenesia new friendship is nearly as easy when you're bombarded with painful blisters on your toes. It's a different kind of distraction that detracts from your ability to enjoy the social experience that is waiting for you.

The feet are the foundation for every Traveler who wants to offer friendship to others. Toughen yourself up. Prepare, so that before you speak peace, you're living peace. Before you seek friendship, be friends with yourself.

Chapter 6

Assumptions

Never attribute to malice that which is adequately explained by stupidity. -- Hanlon's Razor [14]

Perhaps we can assume one thing: that at their very best, people are stupid, or at least ignorant or incompetent. At first crack, this sounds like quite a dig at my fellow humans, not a friendly thing to say! But consider it in the context of a budding friendship.

Other people are ignorant of your inner turmoil. The butterflies you get when your crush walks into the room—your crush doesn't know, your crush is ignorant. If he or she treats you with what you perceive to be scorn, remember: they may just be ignorant. And due to their natural ignorance of the voices that are only in your head, other people are therefore incompetent to communicate effectively with you. Your self-consciousness does not serve you well. Get over yourself, human! Nobody else is thinking about you as much as you are!

I have been stood up well over 100 times for business meetings. Maybe more than 500 times since I began to work for myself in 2009. At first, the blame was on me. I needed to learn how to set an appointment and make sure the other person was on board. For example, when I was in sales I used to say, "Can we set an appointment for ten tomorrow?" And I got a response like "Whenever you want to drop in, I'll be here all day," which doesn't mean the same thing as "I will put your name on my calendar, and I'll be expecting you at ten and have my administrative assistant see you in." Showing up for meetings that were poorly arranged like this got me embarrassing and dishonoring responses like "Who are you again?" and "What was it you wanted?" Which is not a great way to open a meeting, or worse, the assistant might say, "Mr. X is busy right now, if you want to try back in two hours, he might have a few minutes." I could have assumed people were being malicious toward me, but the reality was that I wasn't making a firm enough ask or picking up the blow-off language in the responses.

I heard a story from a friend of mine in Dubai about a fellow who went in for a sales meeting. He got five minutes with the CEO of the firm, with a sign on his desk that said: CEO. When the CEO said, "What can I do for you?" the salesman replied,

"So you're the CEO of this company, huh?"

"No," said the CEO, and the sales meeting was over.

On the one hand, the salesman needs to ask better questions, but perhaps the CEO could be a bit more gracious. Difficult to do when you're on a schedule and someone is, as my dad would say, "farting around". A sales introduction with a major leader is not the place for that!

But the blame cannot always be placed on me: even after the invention of apps that organize calendar meetings for multiple people across multiple time zones, I have been stood up by clients who are paying for my coaching and training.

> "No," said the C.E.O., and the meeting ended.

Each time I exercise the discipline to assume the best: there may be an emergency, they are incompetent at running their schedules, they plain old forgot, I didn't follow up well enough for some reason... occasionally I'm a few minutes late or completely forget a meeting too. I'm not perfect. I'm stupid hundreds of times more often than I am malicious. On my end, the intent to do injury, dishonor or disrespect someone is nil. Why would I not assume that others are equally stupid about how their actions impact others?

How does this play into friendship? "Love is patient." Developing patience comes along with the expectation that sooner or later people will be stupid and forget, ignorant of your feelings, or incompetent to communicate their own feelings. Or, they don't want to have the meeting, so they subconsciously sabotage it with a perceived emergency, but they aren't able to identify the feeling behind not wanting the meeting. For someone like me who is a leadership and life coach, the reasons can go down deep. They're ashamed they haven't done the work they committed to doing, or they don't want to tell me they can't afford to continue financially. The list goes on. None of these reasons are malicious. People out there are suffering their own internal dialog of insecurity, guilt and shame, confusion, lethargy, and laziness. While this means they are mostly just being human. Their issues don›t help to build the friendship, and perhaps even hurt it. This is unavoidable in human relationships, and it is unrealistic to think it will never happen to you.

To be patient, you must have the strength of character to recognize that you're just about as stupid and incompetent as the next person. And are you intentionally malicious when you stand someone up? Generally, you are not. So, if you are not, then assume the best of others. If they start a meeting with a stupid question, you can always say something positive, like, "Could we get to the point? What do you want?" This is a direct approach that will work with most Germans, anyway. And CEOs who are clearly the CEO, because the sign on their desk says "CEO".

Instead of assuming that other peoples' actions are directly aimed at you, realize that they are thinking about themselves just about as much as you are thinking about yourself. And they are thinking about you just about as little as you are thinking about them. Your insecurities are not their problem. Don't make your insecurities someone else's problem by assuming something other than the fact that they aren't being aware. So, you must communicate.

I was so pleased when Sammy introduced herself and said, "There is no reason to lie to anyone on the Camino." She is German. She invites direct communication! I had permission to say what I wanted to say. If I wanted to walk alone, that was okay. Sammy is strong enough to assume that you are taking care of yourself, when you say you want to walk by yourself.

> There is no reason to lie to anyone on the Camino.

We make assumptions about other peoples' intentions every day. I recently heard that there is a saying in Germany that translates to English roughly: "It is time for you to leave, I am feeling visited enough now." The Germans are known for this sort of abruptness. There is a directness to this sort of communication that shocks people from other cultures. But there is something admirable in this method of communicating, too. In indirect communication style cultures, there are ways of letting people know so that they don't need to make assumptions, too. I'm not as adept with them, but the bottom line is that if you're unsure, you should ask. With someone like a German, you just ask that person. Other cultures prefer to be indirect and take their time getting to know one another. With someone from an indirect communication culture, you might want to ask a mutual acquaintance. "How can I find out if I am overstaying my welcome when I spend time with so-and-so?"

When relating to people from other cultures, not making assumptions might be impossible, but not making assumptions about malicious intent is possible in any situation, because generally people are eager to become friends with others, no matter what their background. I think back to a trip to Senegal in 2005. This was only 4 years after the disaster of 9/11, an event that was still fresh in everyone's minds when Muslims met Christians. I had two distinct conversations. In the first case, a young man approached me on the street in Dakar. After finding out I was an American, he offered a statement to the effect that after 9/11 he felt terrible, so he sent a letter to the American embassy saying how sorry he was for our people. This young man was pro-American and sought me out to tell me so. It was a healing moment for me to have a random young Muslim man offer conciliatory words. In the second instance, I went into a jewelry shop in Louga, Senegal, to buy a gift for my wife. An older gentleman came into the shop and frowned at me and called me "Toubab" multiple times (this is the Wolof term for "White man" but can be used as a derogatory term for whites, with the same vehemence that the "N" word is used for black people in America). I was with another American who said, "We should leave immediately." The shop owner wasn't happy; he had lost a sale. Others around the old man were trying to dissuade him from his aggressive behavior, but they didn't or couldn't do much to calm him down because he was an elder. Since he came at me with significant, clear hostility, we hurried away without making a purchase rather than cause a scene. I think the shop owner or manager wasn't happy about that!

These two stories illustrate that often people will approach you with a specific invitation to friendship, a friendliness that will surprise you. In all my travels, the man who said "Toubab" was one of the few who was openly hostile toward me. I have no idea what assumptions he was making about my intentions or purpose for being there. I think I would prefer open hostility over someone planning to follow me and mug me when I let my guard down, but this was a unique case and has not happened much anywhere I have traveled.

More Principles

Don't take things personally.

Assume the best.

When someone is hostile, walk away.

When someone is friendly and you're not interested, that's okay.

Don't laugh in people's faces.

You don't have to reciprocate their attention if you don't want to (just because they have a crush on you or want to walk with you on the Camino or whatever, you're not obligated to be friendly) but don't be a jerk about it, either.

Chapter 7

Comparisons

Comparison kills creativity and joy. – Brené Brown

A n old friend of mine named Jason Potsander lives three blocks away. While battling cancer in 2021, in between chemo treatments, Jason "Everested" on a bicycle, which involved climbing over 29,000 feet of altitude in 22 hours (19 hours on the bike with no more than 3 hours rest). He also worked with his CancerBeDamned team to win a fat-tire bicycle gravel road race series in Michigan. He didn't win every race, but he accumulated enough points to take first place for the season. In these races, Jason was riding around 19 miles per hour with a fat-tire bike on gravel for several hours. He's not a professional athlete, but he's a highly respected amateur.

Justin Gillette, another track-and field-alum from my alma mater, Goshen College, lives a block down the street from me. He is 38 years old, and he has won 119 marathons. Only one person in the world, that he knows of, has ever won more Marathons. He's won marathons in 35 states. He doesn't know how many marathons he has entered, nor how many in which he has placed second or third. While his wife was in graduate school Justin ran minor marathons (usually with 2000 entrants or fewer) to earn his living, grinding out small prizes every weekend to make money, like a minor league baseball player or third division soccer player. A simple daily training run for Justin is one hour; he covers ten miles (16 km).

I met Don Gabriel on November 1 in Porto. He was about to start his tenth Camino trek, even as I was preparing to begin my first one.

There are plenty of amateur athletes right around me who did more difficult things than I did last year. While I'm content with what I did, I find no benefit or value in comparing myself to others. I think they're inspiring. I don't need to be like them. I don't need people to think I'm a "monster" or a "beast".

However, *I have* been called a machine by friends who admire how prolific of a writer I am. One day in January 2022, I started the day talking to two aspiring writers, one who has published his first book and is trying to figure out how to sell it, and another who is debating how much authority he wants to give his editor. They are in awe when they think of how many books I have written. At the same time, I see people on the Internet all the time who published three times more than I did last year; twelve books to my four. Ah. Comparisons.

On my last day of hiking, Britt and Jasmine asked me what I thought of those pilgrims who only walked one hundred kilometers (62 miles), the minimum necessary to receive a *credencial*. I said that while I would never do the minimum myself, what of people who took thirty-five days to do the entire French Route, more than double the distance we would walk? What might they think of our two-week journey? Would they judge us for only having hiked three hundred kilometers?

There's no reason to compare ourselves with others. It isn't useful when it comes to friendship. If walking three miles is a great feat for you, walk three miles. If you need to walk 3,000 to get that sense of accomplishment... well, either way, you'd better get started. Because while you don't want to compare yourself to anyone else, you'll always have to compare yourself with yourself.

It's your Camino. Walk it your Way.

Chapter 8

Boundaries

Jesus walked this lonesome valley / he had to walk it by himself / oh, nobody else could walk it for him / he had to walk it by himself.

You must walk this lonesome valley / you have to walk it by yourself...
African-American Spiritual

We're getting around to discussing sacrifice, eventually, but first a discussion on boundaries is necessary. Preparation—toughening the feet physically as a metaphor for emotional toughness—is one key to good sacrifice, and another is healthy boundaries. You can't make a sacrifice if you don't know your boundaries in the first place.

When it comes to boundaries, one consideration is the difference between *bounded set* and *centered set* relationships, which was mentioned earlier. "Bounded set" means there's a distinct border with some people in and others out. "Centered-set" relationships have to do with orientation toward or away from a central point, without anyone needing to determine whether you are in or out.

I do have a bounded-set approach to some relationships. There is IN and OUT in some cases. I learned as a leadership coach to create agreements or contracts. Without one, someone is not my client. They are OUT until they are IN. For another example, my wife and I do not have an open marriage! She is IN, and everyone else is OUT. On the Camino, however, discovering friendships works more like a centered set. There is proximity and synchronicity, being in the same place at the same time. But Santiago is the center— the end point that most travelers are headed toward, so as we approach the Cathedral around the same time, we are facing and headed in the same direction. Healthy boundaries in the centered-set state relate to how I choose to interact with those around me. As Sabrina said, "I went on the Camino expecting to be alone. I was pleasantly surprised to find so many friends!" Being oriented toward the same goal is a huge part of making friends. Those headed the opposite direction weren't as likely to become friends.

I think expecting to be alone is a healthy approach, both on the Camino and in life. Friends will come and go, and while my own marriage is strong, I know that even the most intentional of relationships sometimes falter, let alone those which are not-so-intentional. My wife and I have experienced this. Her best friend from childhood moved to Jerez de la Frontera, Spain, and married a man from Cameroon. In the last 23 years, we have visited them once. My best friend from childhood lives in the Atlanta area, and we rarely talk. In the last 20 years we have seen each other no more than five or six times.

Expecting to be alone is a great starting point because this is a place where you can set aside your self-consciousness and enjoy being just who you are. Then, when you discover others who offer friendship, you have the option to accept or reject them based on your own wishes and desires, rather than out of a desperate need to fill a void— an expectation that you ought to be with others, that they ought to fulfill you somehow. You can accept friendship, for as long as it may last, with joy and peace, knowing that you're inviting others into your circle because you want them there. As much as I am "the friendliest guy" I am also not interested in a codependent friendship where someone needs me to be there for them all the time, to give them security. I am not a bodyguard, and I don't want to be a buddy-guard, either.

Expect and prepare to walk alone.

Take care of your feet.

When it comes to adding friends into your circle, know what you want and what you will and won't do. I'll occasionally have a drink of alcohol, wine or beer with dinner. When they brought liquor out to our Camino group for shots after dinner, I said, "no thanks". That's my boundary at work. Someone at the table said, "What are you afraid of?"

"Nothing. I just don't want one; I have had enough."

Theirs was a bit of a careless remark, and I didn't assume it was meant to be offensive.

But I'm not disrespecting my own boundaries. I must know what is enough for me. Beyond that lies calamity. If my friends think I'm something less because I choose not to participate (and I never got that vibe) then they aren't great friends, are they?

Taking care of your feet is like having healthy boundaries. Your feet must be tough enough to withstand friction, but sensitive enough to feel the rocks. You certainly aren't healthy if your feet are numb... that only means something is wrong.

Chapter 9

Sacrifice

There are two types of sacrifice: correct ones, and mine. – Mikhail Tal

I was sitting in the albergue in Porto after the return bus trip, talking with Sven. We discussed the reasons you might not walk with someone, which I will recap here:

1 & 2) They walk too fast, or too slow.

3 & 4) They talk too much, or too little.

Sven said that about covers it.

Upon examination, later, I think there is more, but those four gave our conversation a solid start.

A woman named Alex asked something like, "but what if you decide to be their friend and do it anyway?" And I said, "Ah, now you are talking about sacrifice. I've been thinking about that..."

The sacrifice bunt in baseball must be a fair ball, it must be in play, within the boundaries of the game. The sacrifice of a queen on a chessboard happens on one of sixty-four black and white squares. You cannot sacrifice a queen that is NOT on the board! Laying down your life for your friend is no cliche. It is the most difficult choice in the world, never palatable, only made tolerable when we have cultivated love. A true friend will go to the end of the earth for love. Like Saint James, a friend will go to Finisterre with you. A sacrifice is a great and terrible adventure.

Love is a strong word, but then, so is sacrifice. They might as well be synonymous. Some modern theologians and philosophers find the idea of sacrifice abhorrent, repugnant, and primitive. You do not need to be a philosopher to know that they are wrong, at least about the abhorrent and repugnant parts. You only need to be an aficionado of chess or baseball to know there is great beauty in sacrifice. Yes, in the ancient practice of sacrificing a lamb or some other animal, there is gore and violence. There is loss and heartbreak. But there is beauty in these painful moments, too. To kill the fattened calf for someone is the sacrifice of future wealth, but it is the celebration of love, friendship, commitment, or the ultimate hospitality in the present moment. Sacrifices mean giving up something you were saving for the future to give something else in the present.

The idea of sacrifice is primitive. I mean that it is an *early discovery of humanity*. Something obvious, something that most likely predates the concept of Zero. The control of Fire. The invention of Ship. The discovery of Path. Sacrifice is not a zero-sum game! I give something up to get something better in return; and I do that not for myself, but for the sake of others, or at least for the sake of us. The earliest civilizations discovered this as a natural law of the universe. A father throws himself in front of a lion to save his child. A mother gives up her last meal during a drought to feed her child. The tribe discusses these acts and finds no other explanation than to say that these sacrifices, born of tragedy, are the noblest things to do, worthy of respect and honor. We depend upon each other for survival, and for one to make a sacrifice so that others can live is a heroic act. It would be difficult to see it any other way, in any culture or civilization that ever existed. Soldiers are revered because they enlist and march forward knowing full well that they may make a sacrifice, a limb or a life or their mental health.

There are two kinds of sacrifice. There are sacrifices where someone or something else is being sacrificed; the one doing the sacrifice is offering something they can manipulate or control. I'll call those pagan sacrifices. And the second type is a holy sacrifice.

Pagan sacrifices are manipulations. In their earliest form they were a tactical attempt to manipulate the gods. While sacking your queen in chess may be a beautiful tactic, it is a tactic akin to sacrificing another person in some way: the pagan sacrifice. Some human sacrifices go willingly, but there are many ways to coerce their willingness, too. In pagan rituals, rhetoric about the bloodthirsty gods insisting on sacrifice created the illusion that there is no alternative but to send up a firstborn or virgin sacrifice "to appease the gods" and therefore save the tribe from drought or famine. In an ancient Mayan ball game, contestants battled for a victory; the victors won the right to give their lives to the gods as sacrifices. If it worked, great. The gods had listened, had been appeased or manipulated. If it didn't work? Repeat ad nauseum until chance lines up in your favor again. Thank goodness all civilized societies have left this behind, right?

But wait! Pagan sacrifice hasn't ended. Aside from literal ritual abuse, more subtle examples also go unrecognized in our "civilization". Rhetoric about enemies that is used to urge soldiers into battle is an evil in the world; the powerful elites say that "communism" or "terrorists" are coming for us! Someone out there has an -ism that provides an opposition to unchecked economic gain, that challenges a claim to power. The young are handed the illusion that there is no alternative but that you, personally, young man, must go to battle to protect your "rights" or "freedom" or any number of causes... as if it were a zero-sum game. If they win, it means we lose. So, someone's going to have to sacrifice for us! Who will go to war?

I don't understand this. How many people do things because other people think they should? Or think because someone else is taking a risk, they ought to take that same risk, as if to prove something of courage? Doesn't it take more courage to say, "That is not the path for me?" To set your own boundaries and do your own thinking? To say 'no' to the rhetoric delivered by politicians, usually for the sake of some broader economic greed? And if your sacrifice is complete, or if you come home wounded in body or spirit, will you benefit? Or will it be only those powerful elites who convinced you that the battle was worth fighting who benefit? But the tribal rhetoric, the pitting of us against them, is a powerful force for evil in the world, by which the powerful can coerce the populace to sacrifice themselves in a pagan ritual.

By the time you discover the reality of your situation in a moment of clarity, a moment of disillusionment, when the spell cast upon you falls away from your eyes, it may be too late. Your neck is on the block, your heart is in the hands of the priest. Your ass is in a foxhole, you've wet yourself with fear, your best friend is bleeding, and there's no getting out, you want your mama, and all you can say is "F*ck it all to Hell." Defiantly, you rise up and fire your weapon at the enemy, who is only wishing that he were at home with his mother as well, and you blaze away until you're dead, or you jump on the next grenade to save your brother in arms. Doesn't this happen in every war film? And the sacrifice is applauded by the audience. "That guy laid down his life for his friend! Yay!"

Disillusionment: The realization that you have become a pawn, leverage in someone else's sick game, their brokerage for gain and wealth, for power and authority. They have already sacrificed you, and your only hope at some sort of redemption is to save the life of your friend. I don't know from personal experience, but I expect that in that foxhole you experience a sort of instant bond like what I've described as pontenesia. I don't envy you this kind of friendship, brothers, sisters.

This isn't a pilgrimage; this is a bloody war.

So, you lay your life down, but by the time you make this decision, you've been put in a no-win situation, a zero-sum game where you're the predetermined loser. You played the slots, but the casino stacked the deck against you. It looks like self-sacrifice, but we really need to ask: Is this noble? I say No. It is tragic. You are just a pawn on someone's political or religious or economic chessboard. Sick pagan human sacrifices in the postmodern era look like this: 1) you believed a lie, you fell for some rhetoric, and went willingly to the slaughter. Perhaps, against human nature, you killed others on your way. 2) Some chess master considered you a pawn and exchanged your life for something that will benefit them and their families. 3) Some combination of these two. You deserve pity more than honor.

In contrast to a pagan sacrifice, what would be a holy or "whole" sacrifice? You have no illusions. Your hand is not forced, nor is your situation dire. Your choice is yours to make. You have agency. You have the most clear and objective view of the circumstances that could be possible at the time. You make the choice with purpose, on purpose. An example: First responders going into a building at the World Trade Center on September 11, walking into danger to try to get others out. Taking that risk for the sake of others and losing the gamble. On the Camino: You commit to walk with someone who talks too little, walks too fast. You commit to being by their side, and you stick with it. You make a pact of friendship, and it costs you something. Your solitude. In a marriage, it can mean simple things like giving up what kind of food you want to eat, and massive things like where to live. Make this kind of sacrifice, and you deserve respect on top of honor.

Could it be that the earliest groups attributed to the gods a similar reaction to sacrifice: the bestowing of honor, respect, glory, and prestige, as a massive anthropomorphism? Or does God truly see things that way? It is said that we created the gods in our image. It is said that we are created in the image of God. On the old road, I had a good look at the forests and the hills and the rivers and the ocean. We did not create all that — we only created the road to make our travel faster, to connect ourselves with others. So, as ancient travelers saw too, knowing that nobody human had created all they saw as they sailed or walked along, we cannot take the credit for creating gods, either. We only observed that something greater must have made it all, and through inductive thinking we discovered that which always WAS. But it cannot be helped that we only see God from one basic perspective, through one basic lens with our worldview as humans.

If, in our worldview, a sacrifice is beautiful, the height of glory, why would we not also attribute this natural law to something God created as a principle in the universe? This principle states that sacrifices, at least some of them, are holy acts of selflessness. And if God made this a principle of the universe, why would not God also glorify Godself with sacrifice, on principle? The detractors of sacrifice as a core tenet of Christianity consider sacrifice a pagan ritual and have difficulty seeing the difference between pagan rituals and right sacrifices. Was God the Chessmaster and Jesus the pawn? Did he send Jesus the same way Senators send farm boys to die in battle for the sake of whatever economic interests they represent? A few statements that Jesus made [15] indicate how he viewed the issue:

The thief comes only to steal, and kill, and destroy; I came that they may have life...

Jesus asserts that he has no illusions, he is fully disillusioned, aware, and that he acts with purpose

No one has taken [my life] away from me, but I lay it down on my own initiative.

Jesus asserts that he has not been coerced, that he operates in complete agency.

... I and the Father are one.

Here he indicates that the will of the chessmaster and the will of the pawn are identical, completely in sync with each other, purely harmonized, the pawn is the chessmaster. He knows a sacrifice will be made, and he knows he has

authority to lay [my life] down and... authority to take it up again!

The surprise ending. A pure, holy sacrifice bears with it a certain energy which cannot be extinguished. It lives on. It gets passed on. Nobody before or since has made such a perfect sacrifice.

In commentaries on chess, it is often said that "the sacrifice must be accepted." In baseball, if a player executes a sacrifice properly, it must also be accepted. There are sacrifices that are acceptable. If a sacrifice is acceptable, it will be accepted. A common feature occurs in chess and baseball and in pagan sacrifice, as well as the earliest story of sacrifice in Hebrew scripture, that of Cain and Abel. It is a manipulation, a tactic.

But in life, in the very real spiritual world, it is not a manipulation. It is not a transaction. You don't get something back. If something is offered, you ask only that people pass it on. We cannot physically die and take our lives up again, but we can ask for the gift to be passed on, and in this way, we ask someone else to take it up! Yet a pure sacrifice is not a zero-sum game with one winner and one loser. Instead, the world is enriched. Instead of enriching ourselves by giving up someone else, as the Kings and Senators have always done, we impoverish ourselves to enrich the rest of humanity, and something exponential happens.

It was a small sacrifice for him, I am sure, when Jacinto came to Ponte de Lima with my technology kit, which I had forgotten to put in my backpack. Included in the plastic Ziplock bag were a lightweight keyboard that allows me to type on my phone, an extra battery, and all my charging plugs and cables. It was a sacrifice, first of all: a sacrifice I asked for and one I had to accept. For Jacinto, it was a quick, twelve-mile drive, and probably only cost him half an hour. For me, it was the recovery of things I needed that were left behind at least four hours on foot; I didn't have time to trek backward, no idea how to catch a ride to retrieve my possessions, and Jacinto gave me this gift. He drove his car to Ponte de Lima, walked across the Roman bridge and found me at the municipal albergue, delivered my lost items, and said, "I have been instructed not to accept payment for this. If you find someone tomorrow who needs some money or something, give it to them." Perhaps to Jacinto and Fernanda, this was not a big deal, perhaps not even a sacrifice at all. I wouldn't be surprised if they do it every couple of days; pilgrims leave stuff behind all the time, sometimes by accident and other times as they realize they're carrying more than they need. No doubt they get some errands in, perhaps pick up something at the store in the larger town and make the most of the car ride. But to me it was a real gift.

At Casa da Fernanda, every peregrino is a friend, and every day is an opportunity to serve the friends in their community, and every day they sacrifice something, at the very least, their privacy, to do it. The Portuguese Central route is worth traveling just for the opportunity to spend one afternoon and evening with Fernanda and Jacinto. Leave Barcelos early and arrive around two in the afternoon. There is no price set for staying with them. They only accept donations. Give generously!

Assuming the best of others and setting healthy boundaries for yourself creates an environment for friendship and sets the stage for noble and holy sacrifices. You take your boundaries, the ones that help you take care of your own feet and bend them or break them enough to give something up and include your friend out of the wealth you have to offer. So what are the boundaries? They are the limits of self-care that sacrifice intentionally violates.

At the end of the conversation with Sven and Alex, we discussed people who are prone to codependent relationships. How do you choose to walk with someone who walks too slow, talks too much? And what could be even worse? Sven said that he really can't tolerate someone who is afraid to get lost. They need you to help them find the Way. They're afraid they'll miss an arrow. (I suspect he had this exact experience on his Camino.) For Sven, it would be a sacrifice to walk with a person like that, perhaps more than he cares to give. I said, "You could tell them, 'I'll walk with you today, and you'll lead, so that by the end of the day you will to be confident you'll find the arrows tomorrow, because tomorrow I'm walking alone, or with someone else.'" This is not a permanent sacrifice, but a temporary one. When someone comes along who has co-dependent tendencies, your boundaries must be intact. Then, if you choose to sacrifice, you're not doing so in a way that violates who you are and what you're about. Alex and Sven seemed to like this idea quite a lot. You see, we're attracted to sacrifice. We don't like sacrificing too much for people who are weak and unwilling to grow, but we're glad to help them along the way, too. It requires a healthy balance.

We are not gods, therefore we must always return to taking care of our own humble feet, so we can make sacrifices, but we must always remember to set our boundaries. We can sacrifice for a day, but we don't have to choose to sacrifice for someone forever. Once we have made the sacrifice, we can invite them to participate in sacrificial behavior. As Jacinto said, "pass it on. If you meet someone who needs the money more than I do, give it to them."

I found ways to do that on the Camino. But that isn't the end, it's only the beginning.

Chapter 10

Approval and Affirmation

I look ... bohemian! – Megan Fleming

One day after I returned from the Camino, my wife and I were preparing to go out. She got dressed up and I said, "You look nice."

"Don't say I look nice," she said, frowning at me.

"Why not?"

"That's what my mom always used to say when I had to dress up for church." She made a face like yuck. "What should I say instead?"

"I don't look nice," she insisted again, "I look... bohemian." She broke into a grin.

Nice is a garbage word. I am a writer - I should know better! Why am I using the word "nice" at all? *Bohemian* is an apt description for how my wife dresses, to be sure. Nice is an approval word: When I use it, I'm saying that I approve of how she looks. As if what I think matters! (We have been married 23 years... it doesn't.) *Bohemian* is a descriptor that affirms she is hitting the target she wants to hit. Here's the simple difference between approval and affirmation:

Approval is when you do what I want, look how I want you to look, think what I want you to think.

Affirmation is when I acknowledge your success in achieving something positive that you wanted to achieve.

A lot of well-meaning people give their friends approval all the time. Here is the problem with approval: approval is a judgment. It's a positive one, to be sure, but none of us want to be judged, and if we do there's an issue with our ability to take care of our own feet, to walk alone. It's great when your friend approves of what you do, but it can build a codependency; their approval becomes a drug that feeds something desperate in you. And what happens if suddenly one day they don't approve of you anymore? How devastating is that!?

Affirmation, on the other hand, is about seeing someone for who they really are, and naming that characteristic that makes them unique. My wife knows that I don't agree with or "approve" of some of her philosophical ideas. She's currently studying for a master's degree in Comparative Religion and Philosophy. For me, it would be a waste of time. At the same time, I have affirmed her, by saying, "I know your heart. I know you're a loving person. I'll support your study of things that I might not bother reading about. I don't even know how the expense of your schooling will return to us, financially or otherwise, but I am sure you'll find a way to use it." This is my way of affirming her character, rather than approving of her deeds, how she spends her time, or even what she thinks about the Universe.

A good friend focuses on affirming another. Giving your approval, even when positive, is demeaning. "Don't say that I look nice!" There is only one Judge whose approval matters. Why should you have the authority to approve or disapprove of someone else's thoughts or behavior or dress?

Jonathan said to me that there are very few people to whom he is accountable. What I took from that is that he doesn't need approval from a lot of people. He also deals in philosophical thought in his work and comes across detractors on occasion. It's amazing how many people will go out of their way to voice disapproval of his work, but those same people don't hold a position of authority over Jonathan. I've heard those stories over the years from him, and I admire his steady approach. It doesn't seem to rock him very often when people randomly email him saying, "I don't like what you're doing." Jonathan doesn't need my approval, either, but I know he's glad to have my affirmative friendship.

Not every reader of every book who doesn't "Like what the author wrote" is worthy of that author's concern! Kurt Vonnegut wrote some wonderful letters in response to people who thought his books should be banned from their local library or high school reading list; if you want to know how to respond to detractors, Vonnegut's letters are a great place to start. I don't need every reader's approval; desiring universal approval would be unhealthy. One reason many writers get what they think is "writer's block" stems from the fear that not everyone will like their story. How preposterous to imagine that everyone will like your book! How crazy would it be for Sammy to imagine that all Germans within a hundred-kilometer radius will like the fish her restaurant serves? Do I need readers? Sure! Do I need any particular person to be my reader? No. Do I need readers who dislike my work? Yes, I do. The more people who disapprove of my work, the more it will sell!

I recently heard an interview with an edgy comedian from India who was under fire for political comments. The interviewer asked if he'd gotten death threats. "Of course," he said, laughing. "Death threats are compliments." Strong disapproval can be taken as a sort of affirmation! Getting hung up on approval can send you into a tailspin, and you'll enter periods of inability to continue to make creative work. Like my friend Jonathan, we all need to keep the places where we look for approval minimal, maintain boundaries that preserve the scarcity of opinions that sway you, that matter. Choose your critics, or critics will choose you and run you down in the street. Don't be the squirrel that isn't sure whether you want to scamper off to the west side or the east side of the street. If you want to dress in a style known as *bohemian*, go for it!

Offering affirmation, on the other hand, is healthy. And receiving it, too. When Joe said, "You're the friendliest guy on the Camino," he was identifying a character trait he saw in me that was accurate. I accepted his affirmation. "Yes, I believe that's probably true," I said. And I wasn't being arrogant! Joe wasn't saying "It's good to be the friendliest guy" nor was he saying it was bad. He was identifying something that made me who I am, he was seeing me. It is up to me to love myself enough to accept and embrace the fact that "being friendly" is part of who I am. I admire introverts. No, I really do! And I have learned how to enjoy six hours of steady walking alone. But get me back with people when the sun begins to set!

I love that my wife has a certain style she's trying to achieve: bohemian. And I love that she's satisfied when she hits the target, that she's happy in the clothes she's wearing. She is comfortable in her own skin and in her own clothes! I certainly don't mind that her idea of a shopping spree is five items for ten bucks at a thrift store. There's a lot to affirm in her frugality, too. I hope to continue to learn how to affirm my wife without ever saying the word "nice" again.

Chapter 11

Waiting and Going Ahead

There are few things more special in life than to have friends who are waiting for you. Not annoyed when you don't arrive, aren't walking fast, can't get there in a timely manner for any number of reasons. We have been talking about how Old Roads require slowing down. These kinds of friends are just glad to be with you. They have all day for you and aren't in a rush to do something else. They will slow down, too, and wait to be with you.

One day, I walked with Sammy. Sammy was strong but not as fast. A few times she said, "you go ahead, and I'll catch up," but I refused, because I promised her that I'd walk all day together and I meant it. I'm talking about the kind of friend who will wait while you shower so they can eat dinner with you. They will wait for you to arrive at the Cathedral and celebrate your achievement with you. Sammy did this for Britt and Jasmine and me. A few hours later, I did it for Jonas.

There is a subcategory of the friend who will wait. Friends of other friends who will welcome you because of the referral you received, even though they never met you before. That's a special feeling, that you're an important part of a network, and the other people in the network consider their network important enough to wait for you, to meet you. When I came to Mouzo on the 13th, Alfonso and Debee were waiting for me because I was friends with Patti Clewett in Barcelona. They had worked with Patti and her husband Curtis in the past. When I told Patti I was preparing to hike the Camino

Portugués, Patti told me about Alfonso and Debee on the Spiritual Variant. I took the Spiritual Variant partly just for the opportunity to meet Patti's friends! So, I emailed them, and let them know which day I was going through Mouzo. Their friend Don Jose was also waiting for me outside a little chapel, and it was Don Jose who stopped me before I could cruise past. "Do you want a stamp?" He asked in Spanish.

"Huh?"

My Spanish isn't great. I thought at first that he was asking if I wanted to sit. *Cebollo* [onion] and *Siéntete* [sit down] and *Sello* [stamp] get muddled in my head especially when mumbled by an old gentleman who has just surprised me and interrupted my walking and my thinking in English. I didn't want to sit, nor did I need a stamp, but from a few yards away, Debee heard my voice (American accent!) and came hurrying around the corner, her eyes eager to meet any friend of Patti's, and she asked, "Are you Adam?"

> The difference between cebollo and sello and sientete get muddled in my head.

It was touching that people who know other people in my network would wait for me. They had gone out of their way to get to Mouzo, where they spend a good amount of time every day during the busy season. They wouldn't have been there during November, because at that time of year there aren't many pilgrims. In fact, Jonas and I were probably the only two people who walked by that chapel that whole day. There's a feeling we get when we come highly recommended to someone else, and they wait to meet us for the first time with an eager anticipation; the old saying goes, mi casa es su casa, my house is your house. Or any friend of Patti's is a friend of mine. This was the only time I came into contact with anyone in three weeks who knew who I was before I arrived. Everyone else I met had no idea what my identity was. They couldn't care less what my profession was, how I was seen within a network, how good I am at my job, whether I'm a good writer or coach or trainer or whatever I do, to them I was just Adam, the friendly guy, and that was great. But one way that you get to access the pontenesia is to meet friends of your friends, somewhere out on the edge of Spain. Or anywhere, really. In a sense, you're already known. The patina extended from the trust I have with Patti to Alfonso and Debee. And thanks to old Don Jose, who was vigilant when he looked like any other ninety-five-year-old fellow who could easily have been asleep in a lawn chair in the sun. He did his job: by asking if I wanted a stamp, or an onion, or whatever it was he said, he stopped me long enough for Debee to run around the corner and let me know I was expected.

Chapter 12

New Friends

For many people, making new friends feels hard. When we're kids and have to go to a new school, move to a new town, or even venture across cultures, this is a common and natural source of anxiety. Will I make friends here? Why are we anxious about it? Because it's important. Babies who are fed but not touched will die. We need human touch, we need friends. It's not just a desire, it's a need. When we become adults, it becomes even more difficult for many of us. Most young adults head off to college or the workplace without being well-equipped for courtship. (That's a topic for another book.) Our old friends tend to become our only friends; we move across town or across the country and some of us have children and others don't and the next thing we know we're all grown up and we think about our circle of friends and realize we don't see each other much. If we're not careful with how we treat them, including doing things like apologizing for wrongs committed and being proactive about keeping some time sacred for our social lives, it's possible to end up being alone and feeling alone.

Totally alone. Yeah, yeah, all you introverts can say it together: "Alone? That sounds nice."

From the way our homes are constructed (in North America) to the way we deal with pandemics, there are many ways in which our lifestyles can create natural and artificial barriers to new friendships. But don't despair. First, other people, even introverts, would like to have friends. Many of them are scared, but they're also waiting for someone to reach out and say hello. If you can become comfortable with yourself, with your own silence, with who you are apart from the things you do every day, you can also say goodbye to the fear of rejection. Even though I've been married for 23 years, I'm still getting better at being comfortable being alone. Walking a lot helps. My wife can't handle the burden of being my only friend. She needs me to go away sometimes and have other friends so she can enjoy being alone. She was happy for me to head off to the Camino!

Once you've gotten more comfortable with yourself, it's time to look around again. Interested in getting to know someone? But how? We've forgotten how to make friends! First, introduce yourself. I'm sorry to have to tell you to do this, but many people don't seem to know that they should, let alone how to do it.

1. Say your name.

2. Give a tiny bit of context. Say where you're from or some other identifier. If you're on the Camino, "I'm from Indiana, in the United States. Near Chicago." Or, if you're at a middle school soccer game, say, "I'm Ben's dad. Ben is the tall kid, Number 7, playing forward."

3. Ask for their name.

And that's it. Start talking and listening. Ask yourself, "What's important to this person right now?" DO NOT ask them for their phone number. At least not right away. Wait until a significant conversation has happened. Maybe you exchanged some ideas for twenty minutes, like I did with Sven; I almost disappeared and then, on the stairs, I asked him to exchange contact information. Maybe you uncovered a mutual interest, like when I learned how excited Carlos would be to go to the Indianapolis 500. Maybe you want to connect later for dinner. If you've seen that there's a mutual interest, you can ask for a number.

I break the rules, but I'm good at this, remember? It turns out Joe is too. I was walking faster than Joe when I met him (he normally walked faster than I did, but he was keeping pace with an Instagram Model from Los Angeles). I came along behind and thought I recognized him, his height, the length and color of his hair...

"Hey," I said, "You're ..." and then I realized he wasn't who I thought he was... "you're not Don Gabriel, are you?"

The first words Joe said to me were, "You're right again! I'm Joe."

Now Joe is a pretty easy name. I found out that Joe has a quick wit even before I found out he was Irish, a fact he certainly wasn't keeping a secret. "I'm from Ireland," he said, as if his accent wasn't going to make that obvious within a minute or two.

> 𝔜ou're right again!
> 𝔍'm 𝔍oe.

Sammy, on the other hand, knows that her Serbian name is a mouthful. So when we introduced ourselves, she told me her whole name, and I repeated it back as best I could, and then she said, "Everyone calls me Sammy, you should just call me Sammy." Since Sammy let it be known that saying her full name wasn't important, I stuck with calling her 'Sammy'. Sammy is a Serbian passport holder whose parents immigrated to Germany. The first thing I learned about her was that she believes in telling one another the truth. And so, we did. A friendship was born.

I would be happy to learn to say someone's name, like my friend Atef in Cairo, whose name really isn't spelled with an A as we know it in English, but with the Arabic vowel Ain, (a vocal sound unique to Arabic that sounds a bit like you're swallowing a frog while trying to say a short 'A' sound). When the Arabic language is written in what they call the Franco alphabet (the same as the English alphabet) the Ain is written with the numeral 3. My friend's name is really "3tef". Anyway, it's interesting and hard to say, for me. But I think this is a key, important feature of introductions. Ask someone to say their name a few times, repeat it back. Make your tongue and throat do yoga and try your best to imitate foreign sounds for foreign names. People will appreciate it. There's nothing we like more than hearing our own names spoken out loud, even if incorrectly, so long as we know someone is trying.

I've been called *Adamsss* in many countries. Where they are getting the S sound I'll never know. But I'd rather be called that than "Aaron." Aaron is my *brother's* name!

I discovered that imitating languages is a party trick I can sort of do. Somewhere out there, Jasmine has videos on her phone of me trying to repeat phrases in Dutch.

Jasmine and Britt insisted that I was saying these tricky things *"just like a Dutchman!"* I figured it was all flattery, but the ladies were having fun getting me to say Dutch and German phrases, languages I speak not at all.

If you go into it without inhibitions of sounding silly, it's amazing what you can reproduce.

Try to say people's names.

Jonathan and I talked about this. Some people overdo that. It's like they read *How to Make Friends and Influence People* and made it a habit so much that it becomes disconcerting and awkward.

So now I just want to say this directly to my friend: Hey Jonathan, thank you, Jonathan, for that funny conversation we had, Jonathan, about using people's names too often, Jonathan. That was awesome. I laughed so much!

Here's how I introduced myself on the Camino. "My name is Adam, I am from Indiana in the United States, my home is near Notre Dame University, if you have heard of that, or near Chicago, if you know where that is. No? Well, never mind, it's in the middle of America. Nice to meet you."

And that is the beginning of friendship.

Why should I care how well people know their American geography? Could you point to a blank map of Germany and tell me where Stuttgart is?

Reply with your own brand of humor. Don't waste time trying to impress people. It doesn't work on the Camino, and while you might fool people in other places for a while, it's not worth it. When I asked Joe if he was not Don Gabriel, he said, "You're right again!" I appreciated the fact that Joe gave me the benefit of the doubt, that he would assume that I, a stranger, was usually right. Joe put the Improv Theater principle "Yes, And..." to good use. Even if you're uncomfortable, try to have a little fun when meeting people. Make a game out of it in some way.

> Do you know where Stuttgart is?

And there you go. When someone introduces themselves to you, try to say "yes, and." Try to assume they're usually right, usually honest, usually worthy of friendship, and they're going to treat you the same way.

And what if they don't want to spend time with you? If they say, 'No thanks," it's okay. You can be by yourself. And if they say yes? Don't fall over backwards trying to prove to them you're worthy. I'm telling you right now: You are worthy because you're human. This is my personal vision statement— everyone in the world ought to have at least one good friend who can spend time with them without judgment. You are worthy of friendship. You can offer a listening ear and a cup of tea. And you can accept a Christmas gift even if you didn't give one.

Perhaps one of the most pleasant things about the Camino is that you can go with no expectations. On her birthday, Sabrina said something like, "I was prepared to walk this entire way alone. I'm pleasantly surprised to find so many friends here." These two things seem to be at work simultaneously: the lack of expectations brings a lack of pressure. And the slowing down process itself creates space for beautiful surprises.

This means that if you go on the Camino, you also should take no expectations. Don't expect that your Camino will be like mine! You won't have the same mix of unique people I had, naturally. But if you approach it with the same attitude, I am confident you'd get similar results. Why? Because other peregrinos like Roberta, Jonathan, and Sven confirmed for me that this works the same on different routes or at other times, always with different people.

It is said that we only have space in our lives for about 30 deep relationships at one time. I believe this is true. My new friends became that community while I was on the Camino. This doesn't mean that we've all kept touch. As I write this paragraph, it has been about 17 days since I returned from Portugal. Someone messaged me today, but it's early. I don't expect to hear from people often.

Adam G. Fleming

Was it a waste, then, to make these new friends, if I'm not going to invest so deeply in them long term?

Not at all.

Friendship cannot be wasted. Friendship is an end to itself, not a means to get something else. If you can be friends for a day, you can enrich each other's lives.

Jack and Kaya, the married couple from Hawai'i carrying their son Max on the Camino, told me the story of how they met while hiking the Appalachian Trail, or the ""The A.T." as those in the know call it. They had only hiked one day together. Then Kaya went on, because she was a faster walker. Only after they had both finished their walking did Kaya end up visiting Jack in Boston, and the rest was history. New friendships are laden with potential, like the sprouted seed of a tree, they could be crowded out by the rest of the forest of your relationships, but there may be a clearing where they can flourish, too. You just never know. They took their newfound friendship to the Max, one might say!

My friends are welcome to visit me in Indiana. If I wanted to go to Germany or Ireland or Portugal again, I'd have a local contact and I know they'd happily show me around their hometown for a day.

Any frequent traveler knows the value of a local contact. The local contact gets you into the venue you didn't know was there; the tourist brochures and even the travel bloggers who've been there before don't know about that venue! New friends Alfonso and Debee were a great example of that. They took me to a furancho where the host fed us ham and a Spanish tortilla.

Back in 2013, in Jerez de la Frontera, my wife's expat friend let us know about the new flamenco club opening up, perhaps the greatest evening of music and dance I have ever experienced.

New friends are filled with the potential for exposing us to new experiences. Whether we keep in touch or not, we can still say, *That was not a random brush with destiny*. Now I know that person. I know their name. I know their nationality. I know

84

their personality; if they are quiet or boisterous, steady or excitable, driving or relaxed. And I know they know me. Now that we know each other, and we are friends, anything can happen.

In December, Jonathan asked me an important question. "What happens when you go on Old Roads with Old Friends?"

What I saw along the Way, whenever I encountered groups of four people or more, is that they were not having the same experience. I don't know if they get to the noncussions or not. I don't know if they experience pontenesia. But when it comes to pairs: husband and wife, or two old friends who have chosen to walk the Camino together, it's possible for them to not be an insular group. For example, Britt and Jasmine, who came on the Camino from The Netherlands together and stuck together the whole time, sharing hotel rooms, were still open to spending time with lots of new people.

I will have to wait to answer Jonathan's question until I can walk the Camino with three old friends. That may be my next adventure, and something to consider for a future edition of this book.

An Old Irish Blessing for New Friends

(Revised for Joe, Sammy, Sabrina, Britt and Jasmine, Jonas, Alberto, and Hugo, and Jonathan, and the rest I have named; for the hosts serving at the albergues and the monks and nuns praying at the monasteries; for pilgrims everywhere, whether on the Camino or not; for readers who cannot walk; for bohemians, travelers and wanderers, and even for thieves who are hanging on the crosses of their own consequences, still hoping for Paradise).

May the Old Roads rise to meet you,
May the wind be ever at your back.
May the sun rise warm upon your face,
May the rains fall soft upon your fields.

May you know what Enough is when you eat and drink,

May you lay down unnecessary burdens and carry easy packs.

May you experience noncussion as you walk and read.
May pontenesia birth new friendships as old as mountains, as deep as the sea,
As fragrant as a plum blossom, as steady as a Roman bridge across a river
So that you will never forget.
May you find the golden arrows in your heart and follow them.
May the boundaries you set increase the value and power of your sacrifice.
May your sacrifices be pure, passed on, from here to Finisterre.

And until we meet again, my New Friends,
Always take care of your feet along the Way.
Choose your own Camino, while believing in the best intentions of others.
May God hold you in the palm of His hand.

Glossary

Agency. A person's belief in their ability to accomplish an act. Agency differs slightly from self-efficacy. Agency includes the idea that the person's belief is founded in reality, as opposed to somehow delusional. If I said, "I am going to become a famous basketball player in the NBA at age 48," that would not be agency. A term from academic psychology I learned from Dr. Steve Barlow.

Bounded Set/ Centered Set. Bounded set thinking is like a fenced-in field and focuses on who is in/outside of the boundaries, who is good or bad, right or wrong. Centered set thinking is like a field without a fence and focuses on whether people are oriented toward or away from the central point, for example, a well for watering animals in the center of an unfenced pasture. Bounded set says, "do you believe what I believe?" It is exclusive. Centered set, by contrast, asks, "what direction are you facing?" and is inclusive. Paul Hiebert, Fuller Seminary.

Hanlon's Razor. "Never attribute to malice that which is adequately explained by stupidity." Likely named after Robert J. Hanlon. This heuristic, while ironic, applies to a more positive way of viewing the world: believing the best in others. Wikipedia notes a few other similar examples:

"Misunderstandings and lethargy perhaps produce more wrong in the world than deceit and malice do. At least the latter two are certainly rarer." Johann Wolfgang von Goethe, *The Sorrows of Young Werther (as translated). 1774.*

"Let us not attribute to malice and cruelty what may be referred to less criminal motives."-Jane West, The Loyalists: An Historical Novel, 1812. "You have attributed conditions to villainy that simply result from stupidity." Novelist Robert A. Heinlein, Logic of Empire, 1941.

"[Charles DeGaulle's] insolence ... may be founded on stupidity rather than malice." Winston Churchill corresponding with King George VI, 1943. Don't give the Devil credit for things he didn't do. –Adam G. Fleming, 2022.

Instagram modeling. The ironic act of stopping to showcase for other people what a great job you are doing at just being, in a way that distracts you from just being. Especially as an insidious temptation for coaches or people who need to "do self-care" but also feel the need to constantly market themselves.

Lindy effect. The idea that the older something is, the more likely it will continue to exist into the future for an equivalent amount of time. Applies to nonperishable items: ideas, things like books (The Bible) and roads (Via Romana XIX). The Lindy effect does not apply to humans or apples. (If you have lived 75 years you do NOT expect to live another 75 years). As described by Nassim Nicholas Taleb in *Antifragile.*

Noncussion. An event with the head-clearing space, away from social media and other input, often instigated by slowing down on old roads. Original to this work.

Pontenesia. The new friendship with authentic old patina that emerges when Travelers connect during a noncussion. Original to this work.

Sonder. The realization that each random passerby is living a life as vivid and complex as your own; while you also are like an extra in the movie of their lives, stopping as you pass by for five minutes to get coffee in the cafe where they work every day. I apply this as a realization that there are travelers I met so briefly I only spoke a few words, or maybe learned their name but I didn't have a significant interaction with them. From the Dictionary of Obscure Sorrows, John Koenig

Traveler. All humans. Ideally, a human who takes or receives what they need from the environment with a decent grasp of what they need, what they want, who they want to become and where they want to go. Can refer to the human's mental and/or physical state.

Thief. A Traveler or Wanderer who takes more than they need. Thievery can be momentary or consistent, and can be manifested through both a mindset or an active state.

Wanderer. The mental state of a traveler when lost, unsure what they need or want, who they want to be, or what they want to do. In the physical state, unsure of where they are physically going. Susceptible to inadvertent thievery.

Zoom with your Feet or Slow Zooming. The act of reframing one's life, both taking wide-angle views and close-up views, by going on a walkabout. Inspired by photographer's technique.

Appendix I: Chronological Journal

Overview: Beginning at the cathedral in Porto, I walked the Central Portuguese route from Porto to Pontevedra, then veered to the west to travel the Spiritual Variant across the Ríasbaixas municipality of Galicia, which is on a peninsula sandwiched between two bays of the Atlantic, the Ría de Pontevedra to the south and the Ría de Arousa to the north. I made my trek during the off-season, so I was not able to procure the traditional boat ride from Vilanova de Arousa to Pontecesures, which meant that I added 35 km (22.8 miles) on November 14 and arrived in Santiago de Compostela on the following day. John Brierly's Guidebook (A Pilgrim's Guide to the Camino Portugués) indicates the route I took, including detours, was 345.8 km, or 214.4 miles. I have calculated this in different ways, so my numbers may not always add up. Included below is a day in Porto at the end of my trip which adds an additional 13.6 miles, and even if we don't count the few miles I walked around during my days off, I'm sure that I walked at least 228 miles in 18 days.

October 31: drove to Chicago suburb, parked at Coach Susie's house, took Uber to O'Hare airport, spent $120 on a last-minute Covid antigen test: negative; I boarded for Madrid.

November 1: Arrived in Madrid early in the morning, flew from Madrid to Porto, gained an hour back, took a bus from the airport to downtown, found the Cathedral and got my first stamp, walked to Porto Pilgrim's Albergue, arriving around 2:30 PM Portuguese time. Met and had supper with Don Gabriel. Total walking from Bus to Cathedral to Albergue in Porto; 3 miles.

November 2: My only rainy day. Walked from Porto Albergue to Monastery at Vairão, mostly alone. Shortly after breakfast, I met Jack, Kaya, and Max on the road, occasionally walking together. Max was only 18 months old, so he needed frequent stops to eat, play, etc. The couple were such strong hikers that they would stop to feed Max and then catch up with me again. They arrived at the monastery in Vairão about ten minutes after I did, and we chatted throughout the afternoon and evening. Porto to Vairão, 14.7 miles

November 3: Clear skies from here on. Started with Riccardo, whom I met at the Monastery, and we walked together for a few kilometers before finding Igor and Gustavo. The four of us traveled together, until Carlos joined our group in the last 2 hours or so of walking. We encountered Jack, Kaya and Max a few times, but they stopped before Barcelos and I didn't see them again, although I met other people who had seen them. Everybody heard about Max! I wouldn't be surprised if he was the youngest pilgrim on the Portuguese Camino in all of 2021. We walked a long day and ended up getting to Barcelos after dark. Walked from Vairão to Barcelos. 19.3 miles..

November 4: Riccardo long gone, Carlos still in bed, I walked alone, detouring to the west. After a rainy day and a long march on the second full day that was quite tiring, I got into a groove. The weather was nice, and it was about half way through this day that I learned how to really slow down. On this stretch I encountered a guy from Nottingham and a couple from Alaska. The couple from Alaska seemed to be racing the Camino. I pushed to catch up to them for almost an hour, maybe four hundred meters behind and gaining, but after chatting with them for a minute they found another gear and left me in the dust. That was when I learned to take it easy. Not that I was walking slowly, but I wasn't ever pushing after that. I was not going to race to catch up with people. I figured out what my groove pace was, and I wasn't going to walk faster than that, but maybe slower. I also reminded myself it is ok to stop and take photos. Later— when I was taking photos— Carlos caught up with me, we ate some beans and olives and Carlos ate a snail that was in the olives, then he moved on with his clunker bicycle, and I walked a bit with Gustavo until we arrived at Fernanda's. Gustavo and Igor moved on after they took a short break at Fernanda's, where I opted to stay. I was cutting the Barcelos to Ponte de Lima stage into two days. The younger guys were eager to get the kilometers in. I didn't see Riccardo, Igor, Gustavo or Carlos again. The people I met on day 1 and 2 were gone for good. But because I stopped at Fernanda's, I met Sammy, Maya, Esse, Sabrina, Britt and Jasmine and a few others I didn't get to know very well.

Sammy suggested that we walk together tomorrow, and I said maybe. This stage went from Barcelos Municipal Albergue, with the western detour that added a few kilometers, and on to Lugar do Corgo, Casa da Fernanda. 13.6 miles.

November 5: Up early. I decided not to wait for Sammy and walked alone. I saw nobody until after I ate lunch in Ponte de Lima. The others from Fernanda's caught up with me in Ponte de Lima, some decided to continue after lunch, and I didn't see most of them again. In the evening, Fernanda's husband Jacinto and her daughter brought my keyboard, battery and charging equipment to me, which I left by mistake. He refused payment and said to pass on the help or money to someone in need. Sammy and I hung out together, ate a simple meal with some bread, cheese and fruit, and took pictures of the bridge. I fell on my rear in the mud trying to climb on the Roman general's horse. I agreed to walk with Sammy the next day. Easy day, from Casa da Fernanda to Ponte de Lima, 11.1 miles.

November 6: Walked with Sammy all day. After 3 or 4 km we found a place for breakfast. A few minutes after we ordered eggs, I saw the proprietor returning to his cafe with a frying pan. I guess he doesn't make eggs that often if he keeps his pan at the house. We met Joe on the trail, as well as a couple from Los Angeles who were meditating and being Instagram models so I never got to know them much, although I talked with the woman a bit, long enough to find out she was some kind of life coach (funny, I take my career seriously but when I meet other people who call themselves coaches I'm always a bit dubious, especially when they are also Instagram models; I have to remind myself that it is their Camino). Sammy and I also saw a family of 4 from England, we passed each other several times. Perhaps our most significant moment was at the Cruz dos Franceses as we approached the peak of Portela Grande. She was chattering away as we took a break at this cross marking the place where the Portuguese had ambushed Napoleon between 1808 and 1814. I turned to her and said, "do you hear that?" She replied that she didn't hear— anything! I said yes, let's be quiet here and listen to The Nothing. She later said it was one of the most important moments of her Camino. Sammy and I made it over the crest at 405 meters together, the highest point on Camino Portugués Central. Had dinner with Sammy, Britt, Jasmine, and Joe. Sammy and Joe were the only other pilgrims in my albergue that night. Ponte de Lima to Rubiães, 12.5 miles.

November 7: Walked alone again. Nearly turned an ankle on some loose rocks coming down a hill, glad I had my trekking poles. Before I came to Valença, I was taking a leak in the bushes when some dogs started running around and I heard a double shotgun blast just a few yards away. I thought I was going to die. They were hunting grouse or something. Encountered few pilgrims, except the family of Brits who asked me where my "partner" was, and I told them, "Oh, Sammy's not my partner!" and I also saw a fast-walking Mexican guy who caught up with me just as I crossed the river into Spain. He was gone a few minutes later. Pleased to find Joe ended up at the same albergue again and I had dinner with him in Tui. Rubiães to Tui, 13 miles.

November 8: I left alone in the morning, encountered Alberto after 3 miles or so when we both stopped for coffee just after the Puente das Febres. Walked the rest of the way with Alberto. We got to town early (before the albergue opened) and went to a grocery store to find some lunch stuff. Joe caught up with us shortly after we arrived at the O Porriño Municipal Albergue, where Alberto and I stayed with a few other people. Dinner with Alberto and Joe. Tui to O Porriño, 12 miles.

November 9: Sabrina's birthday. I had not seen her since she left Ponte de Lima with some other guys she met at Fernanda's. Sabrina and Sammy had invited Hugo to share their room with them in O Porriño the night before. We Celebrated with Sabrina at breakfast with Sabrina, Hugo, Sammy, Britt and Jasmine. Then I walked with Hugo from O Porriño to Redondela. Joe blew past us while we were having a snack. Joe always started later than I did and walked faster. Hugo went on beyond Redondela. It was during our dinner in Redondela with Joe, Sammy, Sabrina, Britt and Jasmine when I raised my glass "To old roads and new friends." Alberto was at my albergue again, so I hung out with him some too. Another easy day. O Porriño to Redondela, 10.1 Miles.

November 10: I began by walking alone. Joe caught up with me when I stopped for breakfast in Arcade. I was still walking with Joe when we arrived in Pontevedra. Joe had booked a hotel and went straight there, while I wandered, not sure where I would sleep.

As fate would have it, I ended up in the same hotel as Joe anyway and had dinner with Joe and Sabrina. Somehow, I managed to have dinner with Joe five days in a row, which never lacked for entertainment. I failed to connect with Alberto, who was at an albergue across town somewhere. Redondela to Pontevedra. 13.4 miles.

November 11: At this point it had been quite a while since I'd done more than 14 miles in one day. Even so, I took a rest day in Pontevedra, the largest city between Porto and Santiago. Visited the art museum, two churches, and the park. As I left the Basilica, I heard Sammy calling to me from fifty meters away in her unmistakable German accent, "Haloooo, Adam!" So, I met up with Sammy, Sabrina, Britt and Jasmine, who had also decided to take a rest day, to my surprise, and we had a lot of good laughs at noon and also in the evening when we ate pizza together. Alberto and Joe didn't take a rest day, so I didn't see either of them again. I said goodbye to the women, because they were continuing on the Central route, and I was not. Wasn't sure if I'd see any of them again. As it turned out I did not see Sabrina again, but I did see the others. Walking around Pontevedra, art museum, basilica, park: 3 miles.

November 12: I left Pontevedra and after about 3 km I took a left turn on the Spiritual Variant. I got tips from Alberto, who was a day ahead, via Whatsapp: wear long pants, there is gorse. I saw one person who caught up with me as I looked at the sign where the Spiritual Variant diverged from the Central Portuguese way. She went right and I went left (sonder). I climbed from shore of the bay at Combarro all the way up to 460 meters (1500+ feet), then back down into the valley at 300 meters. In the mountains I saw a few loggers, otherwise nobody. I arrived in Armenteira alone. I thought it was possible there were no other pilgrims on the Spiritual Way, ate lunch, went to look for the albergue, encountered the Polish kid for a few minutes, but he moved on. I took a nap before I attended the vespers at the monastery, ate alone, and returned to the albergue where I found Jonas, the professional actor from the Czech Republic, who was eager to have a friend the rest of the way to Santiago. We were the only two pilgrims in the albergue that night. Pontevedra to Armenteira, 14.5 miles.

November 13: I left Armenteira alone, just after dawn, on the Way of Water and Stone. Next time I will wait until the sun is up a little higher, even just an extra half hour, because the first five or six km of this stage are worth seeing in full daylight. I saw some local weekend hikers but no pilgrims. Don Jose, Alfonso and Debee were waiting for me in Mouzo. Alfonso and Debee are friends of my friend, colleague, and coach Patti from Barcelona, so they prayed a blessing for me at a chapel where they often meet and pray for pilgrims, and because I know Patti, they took me to lunch at a furancho. They gave me a bottle of Albariño wine and told me to carry it to Santiago to share with friends. I caught up with Jonas on the beach one or two kilometers outside of Vilanova de Arousa, and we stripped to our underwear to take a dip in the Atlantic... for three minutes. The weather was fair, but the water was cold. Jonas and I ate mediocre burgers for dinner. We met Richard and his wife, I forgot her name, and a South Korean guy at the albergue, they had already been all the way from northern France to Santiago and were headed south to Fatima in Portugal. The albergue was run by the local police. They locked everything down, it was a little overkill since there weren't any of the party-crowd types they get in June, but they were nice about it. Jonas and I were the only northbound travelers at the albergue, for the second night in a row. This stage started at 300 meters and ended at sea level, which made it easier. Armenteira to Vilanova de Arousa, 15.3 miles.

November 14: Alberto let me know that on the day before he was able to get a boat, which requires at least 8 passengers. But Jonas and I were the only ones headed toward Santiago from Vilanova de Arousa on the 14th, and a one-hour boat ride would cost 120 Euros. Alfonso and Debee told me that we could have taken the train because this section of the route is not required to hike to earn a crendencial in Santiago. However, Jonas and I decided to walk together, because that is the point, and we were not in a rush to finish the Camino. We hiked together until about 4 PM. Jonas wanted to talk with his sister on the phone at the end of the day. For the last two hours into Padrón I walked alone, arriving around 6 PM, nearly at dark, but Jonas wasn't more than ten minutes behind, and caught up to me at the albergue. We ate together in Padrón. The famous peppers were out of season. The pimientos de Padrón are a famous hybrid of small green peppers. Nineteen of twenty are sweet and one in twenty is spicy. Like a game of Russian roulette with your tongue. I would have enjoyed a plate of those! But we got some great cheese and massive sandwiches with plenty of protein at a pub. Not much in the way of hills as we walked along the river, but it was the longest day, by about five kilometers. This is not a bad section to avoid— take the boat if you can— because there are some spots by the harbors along the Ría de Arousa around the towns of Vilaxoan, Vilagarcia de Arousa, and Carril, that smell very badly of industrial and seafood industry waste. There are not a lot of woodland trails, either. Finally, it's just a really long day. Nonetheless most of the day was pleasant enough. I wasn't unhappy that I had walked it, I had a sense of accomplishment. Vilanova de Arousa to Padrón, 22.8 miles.

November 15: I left before Jonas and walked alone for the first 15 km or so. Cruising along at a good clip, I caught up with Britt and Jasmine, a very pleasant surprise, as I had no idea where they were. Hugs all around. We stopped for lunch, and when Britt went to pay the check, Jasmine told me that we were going too fast. She had a group of friends coming from Holland to greet them in Santiago and it was a surprise for Britt. Jasmine was trying to stall, but when I caught up with them the effect was that they sped up! So, I played a prank on Britt and pretended to sprain my ankle, stalling us for twenty minutes or so. We finished the last 11 km together, arriving at the Cathedral in a group of 3, where Sammy and three of Britt and Jasmine's friends from Holland were waiting for them. Sammy showed me her tattoo. Britt pretended to be angry when she found out how I had pranked her to slow us down. We went to retrieve our credencials. Later I went back to the cathedral to welcome Jonas. Jonas and I shared a room in a pension called Los 5 Caminos. This was a boarding house more like an Airbnb, less like an albergue. We had dinner with Sammy, Britt and Jasmine and their Dutch welcoming committee; The restaurant wouldn't allow us to open our own bottle at the table, so I shared my bottle of albariño that I got from Alfonso and Debee with them in the street. Padrón to Santiago, 16 miles.

November 16: After some shopping together with Sammy we said goodbye to Jonas, who was headed back to Brno to be sure to be home for his call time at the theater on Friday. Sammy and I shopped for souvenirs and had lunch together, and since my roommate was gone, I left the pension and found a different albergue, where I rested a while and had a bit of conversation with Roberta from Iowa, whom I gave some Tylenol, and a young woman from Lyon, France, who seemed lost. I tried to give her some encouragement; she spoke very little English or Spanish so I could tell she was not only lost but also lonely and my French is good enough to be friendly. She is my archetypal wanderer. Sammy and I had paella and sangria for dinner. The Dutch women were having a girls' day out, so I didn't see Britt and Jasmine again. I said goodbye to Sammy. It was a sad moment for me. The Camino was over, and I was moving into debrief mode. Walking around Santiago, 2 miles.

November 17: I looked for the French woman at 8 AM, but she wasn't there. I grabbed coffee and walked to the bus station by 9 and bought a ticket to leave Santiago at 10 AM. Four and a half hours to Porto by bus. It was weird to backtrack two weeks of hiking in such a short time. I walked from the bus station back to the Porto Pilgrim's Albergue where I stayed on November 1. I got a private room so I could write and rest, but after I went out to find some bread and cheese, I had a nice chat with Sven and Alex for a half-hour which turned into a great debrief. Sven said it was the most enlightened conversation he's had in months. I thanked him for helping me debrief, too. Walking from Downtown Santiago to the bus station/ Downtown Porto bus stop to albergue. 2 miles.

November 18: I left my bag at the albergue and walked around Porto, all the way to the fort on the Atlantic at the mouth of the Douro River, about five and a half miles, and then back. I visited the palace garden and the modern art museum. I picked up my bag at the albergue in the afternoon and got a Covid test so I could reenter the USA. Before it got dark, I walked 2 or 3 miles over to my hotel, the only room that was pre-booked before I left the USA. Hugo, who walked with me on the 9th and lives in Porto, picked me up there. We drove to a cool local spot where we had a sandwich together and chatted about the Camino. Hugo gave me a bottle of his family's port wine as a parting gift. Walking around Porto and later from the albergue to the Covid test and over to the hotel, (why take a taxi when walking another 2 miles is no big deal?) 13.6 miles.

November 19. Rising early, I got a cab from my hotel to the airport. I flew from Porto to Madrid, sprinted through the airport just in time to board my plane to Chicago, took an Uber to my car at Susie's house, and drove home to Indiana, back to my family around 8 PM local time.

December 9-16. Multiple debriefing conversations with Jonathan Bornman, who did the Camino Primitivo and went to Finisterre, late August into early September. He and Carol stayed at our house for a whole week, it was a wonderful time. I've known them since the late 90's, but I had never seen Carol eat ice cream for breakfast before!

January 4, 2022. Sven and I had a Zoom call to talk more about sacrifice.

Appendix II: Gearing Up

I spent a lot of time reading blogs and watching Youtube videos about the Camino, particularly about what to carry and what not to carry. The goal is for the pack to be 10% of your body weight. For me, this meant keeping it under 20 lbs., but I really wanted it at 18 lbs.

Critical things to note: I was preparing for 50% of my days to be rainy. I expected that the weather would range between 44- and 58-degrees Fahrenheit. This is very much a November packing list; summer would be different. Also, you might have a few different things if you were walking the Camino Frances for 800 km instead of the Portuguese from Porto for only 300 km.

Clothes:

- 3 pairs underwear. (I would recommend 4) There is nothing better in the world than clean, dry underwear.

- 3 pairs Smartwool socks, two for walking, a thicker pair for sleeping (recommend 4 pairs)

- 1 long sweatpants, 1 cargo hiking shorts with a belt, (I had to have the belt because I had already lost weight in training and the shorts were loose) 1 lightweight athletic shorts for sleeping. Next time I will invest in some trekking pants, but what I had was adequate, although I ended up wearing the long pants every day for the last five or six days in a row. It got cooler as I went north and of course it was nearing mid-November, too. It would have been nice to have a second pair of long pants.

- 2 tee shirts (I would recommend 4, the reason I recommend 4 of everything is that my friend Joe did this and it meant he could do laundry every 3rd day.)

- 1 lightweight sweater, 1 cotton hoodie. (Do not take a cotton hoodie! It takes forever to dry and it's heavy when you're not wearing it. Get a jacket with synthetic fibers that dry quickly.)

- Rain poncho that covers man and pack both. Used 1 day. I got lucky there. Don't rely on a raincoat and pack cover! I tried that one day during a training hike when it poured for 3 hours on me, and found my pack still got soaked. You have to cover everything as one unit. If it rains really hard the rain will run right down the back of your raincoat and get in behind the pack cover.

- Lightweight glove liners, Smartwool, thin enough you can use a touchscreen. Useful for the first hour or two of walking each morning.

- Old baseball cap. Constant companion. Considered throwing it away when a restaurant owner gave me a cap with their logo, but I can't throw away baseball caps. I just can't. Baseball caps either die on a painting project, get blown away when you're riding a ferry across some body of water, or you lose them. You can't throw them out, they're old friends.

- Flip-flops for shower/evening. Considered crocs but the flip flops were 1 ounce lighter. Save an ounce whenever you can.

- Microfiber towel. Pulls the water off you just fine, dries super-fast.

- Handkerchief— useful for wiping dew off outdoor cafe seating, cleaning your hands after eating an apple.

- Sleeping bag with silk liner and silk pillowcase (silk supposed to ward off bedbugs) Put these inside a medium sized trash bag (British: bin liner) to keep them dry.

- 2 cloth face masks (I hate the clinical scent of medical masks)

- Technology: Phone. MoKo Foldable Keyboard (connects to my phone via bluetooth for typing/journaling). Backup battery for charging phone and keyboard.

European adapter, plug and multipurpose cable to charge battery, keyboard and phone. Make sure your phone is not locked so you can get a European SIM card, this was a problem for me, and I was often without Internet. You might read a suggestion in a blog or guidebook that you should not bring your phone so you can really disconnect. Based on all the QR codes in airports needed for Covid testing, I'd say you really can't travel without one anymore, and once you arrive at the beginning of your route what are you going to do? That being said, you can make a folder of the apps that you intend to use and stay off social media! I did use Whatsapp for communicating with other hikers and with my immediate family back home. I didn't see anyone hiking without a phone, but I did meet other people who were staying off social media.

- Med kit: Prescription medication. Small jar Vaseline, slather on feet/toes each morning to prevent blistering. Do it even if you think your feet are tough from training, because once you get a blister, you're stuck with a blister for a while. Tums, Tylenol, Pepto-Bismol tabs, benadryl, Icy Hot for sore or tight muscles, tape. I used most of these at least once, and several times gave them to other people. Recommend taking blister care items for most hikers. There is a thing called Compeed. It's good. Someone gave me one when my heel threatened to flare up and I wore it for a few days.

- Toiletries: small comb, toothbrush and paste, dental floss, toenail clipper. Soap and shampoo. 2 disposable razors. To save an ounce I decided not to take deodorant but that was dumb. I smelled.

- Papers: Passport, Credencial (they stamp it everywhere you go to help you prove that you've walked the whole way), cash (Euros and a few USD for when I got home), credit cards for emergency and photo ID, guidebook. There are apps for the phone, but the guidebook is helpful if your battery dies or you can't reach the Internet. I bought the one from John Brierley. I cut out the section from Lisbon to Porto with a razor knife to save 3 ounces. Be radical about saving ounces!

- Bags: 1) Backpack. You must have something with a hip belt. You need 80% of the pack weight on your hips, not on your shoulders. Do NOT try to do this kind of trek without a serious hiking backpack! There are lots of options. I bought a relatively inexpensive one for about $250 and it was fine. 2) Nylon string bag for shopping, walking around without the backpack during the evening, and to use as carry-on bag for air travel. I used this a lot, pretty much whenever I could stow the backpack somewhere secure and wanted to walk around in the evening. 3) A shoulder bag/passport bag for my papers, money and guidebook so I could access those easily without removing my backpack. Used it constantly. 4) Assortment of plastic bags also to keep things dry. For example, after washing socks and underwear, they go in the clean plastic bag. If it rains, you have to double down, with a poncho on the outside of your pack and plastic bags inside your pack to protect specific things. Also, this help unpack and repack your bag without having everything all over the place.

- Small roll of toilet paper. Never used it, but glad I had it!

- 2 water bottles. Some days I only filled one of them, just to keep the weight down. There are fountains with fresh mountain water flowing along the path and it is potable. If you walk in summer, you will need to carry 2 x 20-oz. bottles or at least 1 liter. Or you can get a water bladder with hose that goes in your backpack, it's easier to access but if you walk with another person, they can always reach your water bottle for you, and you reach theirs. Joe had a bladder and hose contraption and he still had to ask me sometimes, "hey, can you reach my hose for me?"

- Hardware store: 6 or 8 Clothes pins, 2 extra-long spare shoelaces in case of breakage, which can double as a makeshift clothesline. With the pins you can clip damp clothes/towel to your makeshift clothesline or even to your backpack to dry out while you walk. This would be handy in summer if you take swim wear and go for a dip in the many rivers, streams, and mill ponds. A small padlock and key for locking my stuff in lockers. (I would not take the padlock. I think it's the only thing I could have left at home.)

- Special small stone from home to leave at a cross or some shrine. It felt appropriate when I arrived in Santiago to give it to Sammy instead. My daughter also gave me a cross necklace the morning I left. I put this on a shrine and bought my daughter a different cross necklace.

- Trekking poles. I bought a $35 pair from Kelty and they were fine. I don't think you need to spend $200, but you do want collapsible ones, and I advise a pair, not a single hiking stick. Even when completely retracted, they are longer than the backpack by a few inches. I was able to tuck them in a side pocket and strap them under some of the tightening ties on the pack, so they rode snug against the pack and didn't get damaged in transit. They saved me from ankle sprains, and they take some of the pressure off your knees.

- Walking shoes. I went with Brooks Ghost Goretex, not really waterproof, and I found that the material around your heel is foam that shred way too easily if you get a small piece of crushed limestone in there for a few minutes. Comfort, cushion and weight, fantastic; durability and water resistance, suspect. I never had a blister, but that's partly due to training and breaking the shoes in before-hand, but also due to a shoe store salesman who helped me for 45 minutes to pick the right pair for my unique and oddly shaped feet. Although I don't like everything about the Brooks, I will use them again on my next Camino. The Camino trails are not so rough that you need heavy boots. Perhaps I would have been more discouraged with these shoes if there had been a lot more rain. They are supposed to be waterproof but there's not much you can do when rain flows down your ankles for six hours and soaks your socks from above.

- Occasional fruit, nuts, sandwiches, extra bottled drinks for a short break time. Don't carry more than what you need for the day!

- Bottle of home-grown albariño wine: I carried this after Alfonso and Debee gave it to me, for about 45 miles, from Mouzo to Santiago. That probably pushed my pack to 20 lbs. By that time, I had already climbed over 400 meters twice, and the rest of the way was flatter, so it didn't matter. All the ounces I saved packing were gone when I started carrying a full bottle of wine!

- Purchased en route: pocketknife. Great for cutting bread, fruit and cheese.

Getting stuff home: You can't take wine through security and onto the plane with you, but you can pack it in a checked bag. I had to do this carefully since a backpack isn't exactly shockproof. My belt and extra shoelaces came in handy when I wrapped two bottles of wine inward toward each other from either end of my sleeping bag, rolling them in toward the middle, then strapped it together with the belt and shoelaces. I packed it in the center of the backpack with thick or hard items, like my crocs, around the sleeping bag to protect it.

This worked well, and unlike the time in 2013 when I tried to bring a bottle of sherry home from Jerez de la Frontera on my first trip to Spain, I did not drop and break them, nor were they damaged in my checked baggage. Because of that previous experience, and because Hugo indicated that his bottle of port was a 30-year vintage from his family, I was careful!

I checked the bag from the beginning of the return trip, and this allowed me to take my souvenir pocketknife home, too.

Appendix III: Training

How much do you need to prepare? I met pilgrims who didn't prepare much at all. I was well prepared. Perhaps even over-prepared, but that's not a bad thing when you're 47 years old.

From the end of April to October 31 I logged about 775 miles. If you can average 4 miles per day, you're going to be okay. But you also must have some longer training hikes. Conventional wisdom says that if you can do 12 to 13 miles (21 km) on successive days, you should be ready.

I decided to make sure to do that, (September 4 and 5, see below) but I went beyond that, too. First, I decided that if I was preparing to do 13 days of walking 20 km or more on the Camino, then I should do an equivalent number of days in training at that same distance, although they were on weekends. Over the final 3 months I made time for 12 days where I could hike at least 12 miles. During the work week I did 4 to 6 miles a day in the last few months, while I did my big training days on weekends— just as people do when preparing for a Marathon. I also made time one Sunday to do an 18.5-mile walk (30 km) to make sure I could handle a long day. That training day, when I walked from my house in Goshen all the way to Shipshewana, was slightly shorter than the Vairão to Barcelos trek and 4 miles shorter than Vilanova de Arousa to Padrón leg, but it was sufficient.

Here are my training totals for the six months leading up to the Camino.

May: 99.5 miles
June: 138.89 miles
July: 133.22 miles
August: 77.02 miles

September: 134.23 miles

October: 169.44 miles

And in November... 246.03 miles total, including mileage after I got home from the Camino.

Here are the 12 longest training days I did, and you can see how I spaced them out over the last few months, increasingly from July until October.

July 6: two hikes, 6 and 6.03, 12.03 miles total.

July 31: four short hikes averaging about 3 miles each (between games while watching my boys at a soccer tournament) 12.14 miles total

August 12: One hike, 12.09 miles total in 3 hours 40 minutes (18:12 per mile) I stopped my clock for a 10-minute break at the 6-mile turnaround point. Even with a break I could do 12 miles in 4 hours.

September 4: two hikes, morning and evening, 13.27 miles total

September 5: two hikes, morning and evening, 13.11 miles total, completing my first back-to-back 12+ mile days with almost 2 months left to prepare. Weekend total 26.38; a bit more than a Marathon.

September 11: Two hikes, 12 miles total

October 3: 18.6 miles total (30 km) in 5 hours 49 minutes (not counting breaks) I also did a "short" 9 mile hike the day before, so my weekend total was over 27 miles on October 2 and 3.

October 9: 12.22 miles

October 10: 12.26 miles (Weekend total 24.48)

October 17: 12.07 miles

October 18: 12.4 miles (weekend total 24.47)

October 24: 12.24 miles.

By the time October rolled around I could always walk 12 miles in less than 4 hours with my pack, even if I included a ten-minute break somewhere. It is quite flat around my home. This took up a lot of my weekends for one month, but the amount of effort I put in training was worth it! I didn't deal with a lot of painful blisters, muscle soreness or fatigue during the Camino so I could enjoy the scenery, food, friendship, and company, and being alone without being distracted by a lot of pain.

Throughout October, whether on these longer weekend hikes or shorter walks during the week, I was walking with a nearly full backpack, acclimating to carrying 16 to 18 pounds, on flat terrain around northern Indiana. I didn't have a good place to work on hiking up and down hills, although a few times I drove to Indiana Dunes State Park and hiked in the sand dunes, in particular I did this on June 24, which was the first time I did over 9 miles in one shot and I did that on sand with a lighter backpack (I had not yet purchased a hiking pack so I used a regular backpack for a laptop). 9 miles in sand dunes is every bit as difficult as 14 miles on normal trails! In spite of my lack of training with hills, the hills on the Portuguese Camino were not a problem. They only go up to 460 meters maximum, so you never have a problem with getting oxygen. You might walk a little slower and take a few more breaks, but I was in such good condition that going up the hills didn't bother me.

What I recommend for those interested in hiking the Camino: if you are starting from scratch and not very fit, start six months before, walking 2 or 3 miles a day and gradually increase to six or seven a few times a week, then to nine or ten miles twice a week, and finally, in the two months preceding your hike, get at least six days where you walk at least 12 miles (20 km) in one day with your pack, and one more day where you hike 18 miles (30 km). 12 days x 12 miles is better! But with six days of 12 miles (20 km), you should be ready to do the Camino. I don't think you need to walk 775 miles in the 6 months before the Camino, but I do think you should at least do 200 to 300 miles of training if you want to have a smooth and relatively painless experience.

It doesn't really matter how fast you walk. You can take little breaks, too. Most of the stages are only about 13 or 14 miles and you'll be able to cover it before dark, that is, if you don't sleep until noon! Some of the things to practice with so that you know you're ready to handle your gear:

How to pack your pack so that the weight is balanced; you don't want it pulling left or right. How to adjust the straps and get comfortable having it on your waist, making sure it rides at the top of your iliac crest, a few inches below the navel. How to deal with sudden rainstorms and how you'll feel if you get wet and have to keep walking. Be tough in training; if you have a training hike scheduled and there's rain or other bad weather, do it anyway. Learn how to use trekking poles to take weight off your knees. Figure out how much water you need to carry.

Preparation is not just a thing to do so you're comfortable and the Way is easy, it's helpful if you want to be able to offer help to others and be friendly. If you're well prepared, you can focus on enjoying the experience rather than using the Camino as a sort of penance and grinding it out in a haze of pain.

If you do want to use the Camino as penance, well, don't train. Get some brand-new boots and break them in while you're on the Camino. They'll give you some nice blisters for sure. Buy your gear at the last minute and don't test to make sure that your kit is rainproof, so that you can make sure to get your sleeping bag good and soaked a couple of times; don't be selective with your clothes and extras and carry way too much stuff. There are plenty of easy ways to make yourself suffer extra if you want to suffer. Just promise me that you won't shed your misery onto every passerby and pilgrim you meet.

With good training and preparation, you can let your past be in the past and be present in the moment.

IN CASE YOU MISSED IT: TAKE CARE OF YOUR FEET

Your feet are everything. Shoes for the Camino can be lightweight, as I mentioned above. They should be broken in with 100 miles of walking. Smartwool socks are critical. Cotton is a bad idea, not just for socks but almost any article of clothing. Break in your shoes, train enough, slather your feet with petroleum jelly, put on your Smartwool socks, and you should be good to go.

Endnotes

---

[i] Machado, Antonio (1875-1939) from Proverbs and Songs, 1917

[ii] De Certeau, Michael, The practice of everyday life. 1984

[3] Sonder. See glossary. John Koenig, www.dictionaryofobscuresorrows.com

[4] James 1:19

[5] Lindy Effect, See Glossary

[6] James 4:13-16

[7] https://www.youtube.com/watch?v=TAGjuRwx_Y8

[8] *I'll Push You* by Patrick Gray and Justin Skeesuck

[9] *Tao Teh Ching*, 46, Translated by John C. H. Wu

[10] Bounded set, see glossary. Described by theologian Paul Heibert.

[11] Matthew 7:1

[12] John Wesley, *Selections from the Writings of Rev. John Wesley* (New York: Methodist Book Concern, 1929), 232.

[13] Patrick F. McManus. (1981). *A Fine and Pleasant Misery. Holt Paperbacks; Fifth or Later Edition*

[14] Hanlon's Razor, see glossary. Article by the same name on Wikipedia.

[15] The four statements in Chapter 9, in this order in the text, are from John 10:10; John 10:18, John 10:30; and John 10:10 again.

CPSIA information can be obtained
at www.ICGtesting.com
Printed in the USA
BVHW030032131122
651758BV00018B/1010